BOX! BOX! BOX!

BOX! BOX! BOX!

The Inside Track of the 2022 Formula One Season

Foreword by Karun Chandhok

GARY JORDAN

pitch

First published by Pitch Publishing, 2023

Pitch Publishing
9 Donnington Park,
85 Birdham Road,
Chichester,
West Sussex,
PO20 7AJ
www.pitchpublishing.co.uk
info@pitchpublishing.co.uk

A CIP catalogue record is available for this book from the British Library.

ISBN 978 1 80150 448 5

Typesetting and origination by Pitch Publishing

Printed and bound in Great Britain by TJ Books, Padstow

Contents

ACKNOWLEDGEMENTS

SITTING WATCHING the 2021 season ending, I felt, like everyone else did at that moment, a feeling of sporting injustice. It just didn't feel right; knowing that an ending felt scripted just couldn't happen in a sport that by and large has always upheld its integrity. Had we really entered a time where the result was made for television? It was hard to believe that was the case, and even since then it has been labelled as 'human error', just like a referee decision in other sports can determine an outcome. We all came away with a bad taste in our mouths.

That evening I pitched the idea of this book to the wonderful team at Pitch Publishing. They took a chance on it, and maybe off the back of that result, and the rising popularity that F1 now has, they believed it was a story worth telling. Yes, it is just one season, and yes, more drama has happened since Max Verstappen has retained his crown, but the Pitch team were behind me and I thank them all for helping me create the book you're reading now.

It is always a long journey when putting the words together and as always I'm forever grateful for the love and support of my family who endured watching races each Sunday. Along the way I contacted many people within the industry and more often than not had little or no reply. The world of F1 is closely guarded and not many from outside the inner circle get to see the literal nuts and bolts. Those that did reply to me with help and advice, I thank you. Big thanks go out to Simon Lazenby and Ben Hunt, who took time out of their busy schedules to talk to me, and to Karun Chandhok who wrote the foreword before the season had started and set the tone.

FOREWORD

by Karun Chandhok

This foreword was written before the 2022 season started, and therefore highlights the end of the 2021 campaign with its highly controversial ending.

The 2022 season is a big one for Formula 1. The 2021 season was one of the most extraordinary years in the sport's history. It was packed with superb on-track racing, fascinating technical and strategic battles, controversial accidents on track and decisions off it, public mudslinging, and high tension between the two top teams as well as some virtuoso performances from drivers outside the top title contenders.

First off, let's deal with the elephant in the room!

Ever since the Abu Dhabi Grand Prix last year, the fanbase seems to have gotten more and more polarised and, in the end, I've concluded that there is no way to ever satisfy some fanatical and irrational people out there. In my personal opinion, I believe a fairer outcome would have been to either throw the red flag when Nicholas Latifi crashed and have a simple five-lap sprint to the flag or, if they chose to use the safety car, as was the case, then they should have left the lapped cars in between Lewis Hamilton and Max Verstappen.

Max would have probably passed the lapped cars before Turn 7 and we would have had an amazing final half lap with Lewis trying to hang on. To select just the five cars between Lewis and Max to unlap themselves made Lewis a sitting duck on the final lap and created the overwhelming feeling that the title was rigged to favour Max.

I don't for one second believe there was any premeditated plan prior to the race to favour Max but actually think that Michael Masi was so focused on trying to finish the race under green-flag conditions and clear the lapped cars out of the way that he didn't fully consider the implications of what he was doing at the end there.

The FIA should have been working hard to rebuild credibility after that weekend but, in reality, they stayed silent on the topic for nearly three months and then have come up with a solution that I don't necessarily think is better.

Michael Masi is a good race director, but the FIA system didn't help him because, rather than allowing him to just focus on the all-consuming role of being the F1 race director, they also added other roles that Charlie Whiting, his predecessor, was doing on to Michael's list of responsibilities. Michael was left to fill Charlie's shoes on the Single Seater Commission as well as fly all over the place to inspect new and modified circuits. I even saw him at Formula E weekends in 2021 on what should have been weekends off. The FIA have announced a new system of two different race directors which I don't actually think is a good solution as it creates more potential for inconsistency but let's see how things play out.

As we head into 2022, we've got the biggest chassis regulation change in 40 years. I was really not a fan of the rule changes introduced in 2017 which made the cars bigger and faster because what they also did was make them more aerodynamically sensitive and therefore detrimental for overtaking. Finally, after several false starts by the overtaking working group, the rule makers led by Ross Brawn and Nikolas Tombazis decided to really focus on creating a clean slate of rules to try and improve the 'raceability'. In true F1 fashion, where the conversation started and where we ended up are quite far apart but, having seen the cars in testing, I'm confident that on the whole the rule changes should achieve the objective of making the racing closer.

Every time we get a big regulation change, the pecking order does get jumbled around a bit. In addition to the pure car design rule changes, we have also seen some fundamental changes introduced to try and even things up across the field. For example, wind tunnel time is calculated on a sliding scale with the more successful teams getting less than those at the back of the grid. This means that Ferrari will head into 2022 with 10% more wind tunnel development time, which could be crucial to their competitiveness particularly in the early part of the season. The cost cap has also been reduced by five million dollars and it's been great to see that all ten cars have got to the Bahrain test looking completely different. There were some concerns from the designers that the cars would all look far too similar given the restrictive regulations but actually what we have is a really wide spread of ideas and solutions on every car.

Heading into the year though, as much as the cars are exciting and interesting to see, it's the drivers that most people tune in for. There are some fascinating dynamics in play for this year and really the most interesting rivalry following on from 2021 is between Lewis and Max. For years we had been waiting to see if Red Bull Racing were going to have a car that allowed Max to use his extraordinary talent to take on Lewis and we finally got that. The 2021 season reminded me of the year we should have had in 1994 when the undisputed current king of the sport (then Ayrton Senna, last year Hamilton) was being challenged by a young, aggressive and highly motivated talent (then Michael Schumacher, last year Verstappen).

Now that the dust has somewhat settled on the 2021 campaign, I've been thinking about their dynamic as we head into the new season, and I actually think there are clear similarities between them and the Alain Prost and Ayrton Senna rivalry from 1989.

When I think about the way Lewis has gone about his racing since 2018, it's ironic that even though he has repeatedly talked about Ayrton being his hero, I actually see more parallels between him and Alain. In recent times, Lewis seems to have changed the way he goes about a race weekend in comparison to his early years. Like Prost used to, there's a huge amount of focus on getting the car set up and dialled in for the race. He no longer looks dejected if he doesn't get pole position because he knows the points come in the races. His engineers talk highly of just how much he has improved his ability to look after the tyres and create flexibility in the race strategies that has allowed him to win races such as Barcelona in 2021 or Mexico in 2019 where he had tyres that were 14 laps older than Sebastian Vettel and still held him off to win.

When you watch on board with Lewis, there's a smoothness to his driving that isn't necessarily as extreme as Prost or Jackie Stewart or Jenson Button but certainly it's much less edgy than the style we used to see in his early McLaren days or what we expected from Senna, Schumacher and now Verstappen.

In a parallel to Senna, Max has redefined the rules of engagement against his competitors on track. There's an edgy, ruthless streak to the way he goes racing. There's the incredible self-belief and confidence of a young driver who knows that he has a God-given talent that only a few people in the history of the sport have ever possessed.

The added dynamic to this whole battle for 2022 is going to be George Russell. The young Brit has earned his place alongside Lewis at Mercedes and this battle is getting me excited more than anything else. Unlike Max, who is clearly established as the number one driver at Red Bull, Lewis is going to have to battle his own team-mate as well as Max and the rest of the grid.

This inter-team battle has all the makings of an Alonso versus Hamilton from 2007. A young, highly rated yet largely unproven talent lining up against the best driver of his generation.

A key difference between Lewis and George in 2022 and Lewis and Fernando Alonso in 2007 was actually pointed out to me by Toto Wolff in preseason. He made it very clear that while Ron Dennis had suggested to Lewis that he ought to spend six months being half a second behind Fernando as an understudy, Toto expects George to be right up there fighting for pole position and win from the opening race in Bahrain. Toto was very clear that after the experience he had with Lewis and Nico Rosberg in 2015 and 2016, he will not tolerate a team that gets divided, where the atmosphere internally turns toxic so his personal management of this dynamic will be fascinating to watch.

George proved last season that he is one of the best qualifiers in Formula 1. The laps in Silverstone, Spa and Russia last year were among the best of the season. It's hard to judge his race pace and tyre management because the Williams wasn't the most competitive car and, therefore, we tend to look at that one-off weekend in Bahrain with Mercedes where he was exemplary.

However, the stunning form Lewis showed in the final part of last season should be a warning shot for George. In the past two seasons, Lewis and Max have raised the bar in terms of consistent brilliance in a way that Michael did 20 years ago. Other drivers can get close to them 'on their day' but across the 22 races it's a tall order.

This could be a big year for Ferrari. The Scuderia have gone for a completely different concept to the rest of the field (apart from Haas, with whom they have a technical partnership) with fairly large sidepods, but it does seem from testing like the overall concept is working. It seems evident from the GPS data they have made a big step with the power unit and I believe that Ferrari have the second-best driver line-up on the grid behind Mercedes and it will be fantastic for the sport to have them genuinely contending for race wins and the title once again. Charles Leclerc and Carlos Sainz are both lovely young men who are motivated and fired up to take the fight to Mercedes and Red Bull.

As I write this on the eve of the season, the most exciting thing is that we genuinely don't know how this year is going to play out. It seems like we should have three teams in contention, but it will also be a year where the cars will develop an awful lot through the season as teams unlock performance.

Another vintage year awaits us!

PROLOGUE

DESERT DEMONS

12 December 2021. Abu Dhabi Grand Prix, Yas Marina Circuit

The sun had long gone down, and the floodlights surrounding the circuit were as bright as the sparks flying from the track as the underside of the cars hit the track and kerbs. The late evening start time added to the drama, and the *Decider in the Desert*, as it had been billed, was close to an end, which also meant the curtain was falling on one of the most enthralling, tension-filled seasons in recent memory. It had been one of the longest seasons, literally, 20 races had passed and entered into the record books, but there was still so much on the line.

Germany's Mick Schumacher was in his first full season in the Haas Formula 1 team, after winning the Formula 2 Championship the previous year. Haas, to be perfectly blunt, were having a nightmare of a season, failing to secure a single point. This was about to continue as Schumacher, son of the legendary seven-time champion Michael, was running off the pace again, and out of the points. On this day his was the only Haas car running, as his team-mate, Nikita Mazepin, had tested positive for Covid-19 before the race, too late in the day to appoint a replacement driver, and had to withdraw. The Russian was also in his first season and was having a torrid debut having retired from five races, with a 14th-place finish in Azerbaijan the best he could manage.

The Haas team had taken an executive decision to practically sacrifice the 2021 season, and look ahead to the following year; this meant the car had next to no upgrades and they were therefore a year behind the rest of the paddock. If it were not for this, the down on their luck Williams Racing team would have been propping up the constructors' table, or at the very least scrapping with Alpha Romeo Racing for the lean points each race. The once-proud Williams team that boasted multiple drivers' and constructors' titles had clearly seen better times, and it was only a week before that they were mourning the loss of their founder and inspirational leader Sir Frank Williams; the outpouring of emotion was clearly evident, and maybe because of this it was one too many races in 2021 for the Oxfordshire-based outfit.

After this race George Russell was Mercedes bound, and had retired early with gearbox failure; they had to rely on Canadian Nicholas Latifi to steer their last drive of the season home. Running towards the back of the field, he was drawn into an intense battle with Schumacher. It was these skirmishes in the middle and at the back of the pack that had made the season so engrossing to watch. Latifi was pushing hard, and Schumacher was defending as if he was holding onto a podium finish, not a fight for last place. The Championship up ahead on the track was being won, and it was going to need something extraordinary to change the outcome.

Then, right on cue, the miracle that Red Bull Racing team principal Christian Horner had said they needed for a race victory, during a live cutaway on television commentary, happened.

Running alongside each other in the middle section of the track Latifi thought he had the upper hand, but Schumacher wasn't giving up his place with just five laps left of the scheduled 58. The gap between the two had been closing steadily over the previous few laps and getting instructions from his race engineer Gaetan Jago, Latifi was in attack mode, but he was running out of time. Jago gave him the optimum overtaking chances and Turn 9 was the most favourable. Spying an opportunity, Latifi went for his move around the outside. Schumacher moved to the right to protect his place.

'He forced me off, so …' Latifi exclaimed over the radio. Two quick replies of 'Copy!' came from Jago; at this point the engineer was fairly helpless in the fight and had to watch as his driver was forced onto the dirty side of the track, visibly kicking, and picking up dirt onto his tyres. Latifi went on, his momentum carrying through the next corners, but this also meant he was racing through the dirty turbulent air that was being left by Schumacher. Then it happened. Coming out of Turn 13 and through 14, the rear of the car slipped away, and at high speed, all the Canadian could do was control his crash into the wall. The rear right slammed hard into the barrier, forcing the car around so that the front left collided almost immediately. The car came to an abrupt stop facing the wall. 'Are you okay? Are you okay?' came the concerned call from Jago. A short pause followed by a grunt, 'I lost it. Sorry guys …' Latifi managed to reply.

Immediately a series of events happened. The track stewards raced on to help, firing their extinguishers over the car as a precaution, leaving their dry powder on the car and over the racetrack. The safety car was deployed, causing an immediate flurry of activity in the pit lane, and also for the media worldwide, as a race, and Championship, which looked to be heading to an anti-climax was thrown into chaos. While this was happening, Jago was on the radio going through the usual checkdown procedures to ensure both the Williams driver was safe, and that the car was shut down properly. It was the end of the race and season for Latifi, but his personal life was to take an even more traumatic turn.

After the dramatic conclusion of the race, and the media had turned their microphones away from the leading protagonists, and how everything had unfolded in those last five laps and 15 minutes of unprecedented motorsport theatre, Latifi was asked for his version of events. 'It was never my intention, and I can only apologise for influencing and creating an opportunity.' Of course, no one really thought that the crash was a well-crafted piece of work that would see an outcome to a Championship in the manner that unfolded; after all, Latifi was a race driver and his instincts were just that – to race. 'I went off the track when we were side by side. I mean, he kind of forced me off, but I guess it's fair racing. Nothing untoward there. My tyres got really, really dirty from running off track and I subsequently made a small mistake and unfortunately crashed. This obviously wasn't how I wanted to end our season, so it's disappointing.'

In a world where instant gratification is at the touch of a button, and like so many incidents involving high-profile sports stars around the world, Latifi was now a target. He had been involved in a racing incident that was purely that. His comments immediately after proved that he had no clear indication that his actions were to throw the sport into a cyclone that wouldn't cease for many weeks, and months. Social media has its obvious merits, news travels around faster than the cars on the grid, and after the conclusion of the Championship, the emotions were running high and those that were in their own battle to defend their favourite drivers now had fresh ammunition. There was an endless tirade of abuse aimed at the Canadian, blaming his Turn 14 crash on the eventual result. It was the spark, but the fire that caught and ran wild was out of his hands.

Over a week had passed since the race, and Latifi had been mostly silent; in fact he had stayed away from all his social media accounts after those first early moments after the race weekend. He had seen enough, and nothing he could do or say at that point would change anything – it may have added more fuel to the fires that the keyboard brigade was lighting under him. On 21 December, just a few days before Christmas when everyone should be feeling nothing but goodwill to each other, he broke his silence in a heartfelt statement that was released on his own personal website:

Hi everyone,
I've purposely been staying away from social media to kind of let things settle down from the events of the last race.

A lot has been made of the situation that came about after my retirement in Abu Dhabi. I've received thousands of messages to my social media accounts – publicly and via DMs. Most have been supportive, but there's been a lot of hate and abuse, too.

I've been trying to figure out the best way to go about handling this. Do I ignore and carry on? Or do I address it and tackle the bigger issue that is sadly a reality when you use social media?

This isn't some scripted statement, but rather me speaking my mind in the hope that this maybe sparks another conversation about online bullying and the drastic consequences it can have on people. Using social media as a channel to attack somebody with messages of hate, abuse and threats of violence is shocking – and something I am calling out.

Going back to the race weekend, as soon as the checkered flag dropped, I knew how things were likely to play out on social media. The fact that I felt it would be best if I deleted Instagram and Twitter on my phone for a few days says all we need to know about how cruel the online world can be.

The ensuing hate, abuse, and threats on social media were not really a surprise to me as it's just the stark reality of the world we live in right now. I'm no stranger to being talked about negatively online, I think every sports person who competes on the world stage knows they're under extreme scrutiny and this comes with the territory sometimes.

But as we've seen time and time again, across all different sports, it only takes one incident at the wrong time to have things completely blown out of proportion and bring out the worst in people who are so-called 'fans' of the sport. What shocked me was the extreme tone of the hate, abuse, and even the death threats I received.

Reflecting on what happened during the race, there was really only one group of people I needed to apologise to for the DNF: my team. I did that right afterwards. Everything else that followed was out of my control.

Some people said I was racing for a position that didn't matter with only a handful of laps remaining. Now whether I am racing for wins, podiums, points, or even last place, I will always give it my all until the checkered flag. I'm the same as every other driver on the grid in that regard. To the people who don't understand or don't even agree with that, that's fine with me. You can have your opinion. But to use those opinions to fuel hatred, abuse, and threats of violence, not only to hate me, but to those closest to me as well, tells me these people are not true fans of the sport.

I'm comfortable enough in my own skin, and I've been in this world long enough that I can do a pretty good job of just letting any negativity wash over me. But I know I'm not alone in thinking that a negative comment always seems to stick out more – and can sometimes be enough to drown out 100 positive ones.

People will have their opinions, and that's fine. Having a thick skin is a huge part of being an athlete, especially when you are constantly in a position to be scrutinised. But many of the comments I received last week crossed the line into something far more extreme. It concerns me how somebody else might react if this same level of abuse was ever directed at them. No one should let the activities of a vocal minority dictate who they are.

Events in the last week have made me see how important it is to work together to stop this kind of thing happening and to support those on the receiving end. I realise I'm unlikely to convince those who acted in this way towards me to change their ways – and they even try to use this message against me – but it's right to call out this kind of behaviour and not stay silent.

To all the fans and people that did have my back during this whole situation, I want to say a huge thank you, I've seen and read a lot of your messages and they are much appreciated. It's nice to know I have so many people supporting me.

Sport is by its nature competitive – but it should bring people together, not drive them apart. If sharing my thoughts, and highlighting the need for action, helps just one person, then it was worth it.

As we look forward to the New Year, I truly hope my experiences after the Abu Dhabi Grand Prix help reinforce that message, and my New Year's resolution is to look at ways I can support that process. Just be kind everyone!

I want to wish you all happy holidays, stay safe, and I look forward to all of us getting back on track in 2022. **Nicky**

Formula 1 racing has many incidents each year that will cause heartache for the drivers and their teams. The sport has been accused in the past of having been too processional – on some tracks that is the case as overtaking is immensely difficult, but rules have allowed for better racing of late. This is the drivers' and teams' want, it's what the cars are designed for, and is in their DNA. So, naturally with more racing you will get more incidents. What we don't need is the drivers that risk their lives in these high-speed collisions not only suffering from the effects of their profession, but also from any attack from someone who feels an incredible conspiracy has taken place – then take to their chosen device, log in, and hurl a constant barrage of abuse, so bad that the receiving end has no choice but to turn their back on the world for days. Unfortunately, Latifi felt the ire of many due to the circumstances of the occasion; he wasn't at fault, and he likely won't be the last to be in this situation.

The drivers are at the forefront of racing – they will take the plaudits, but the sport itself is punishing enough, without the off-track distractions.

Welcome to the world of Formula 1.

BREAKING THE MOULD

TAKING ON the team principal role for the Renault F1 team, having only been in the Formula 1 paddock since 2016, Frederic Vasseur was still a relative novice in the role compared to others along the pit lane holding the same position. He was far from being green around the gills though, with a storied background in Formula 3 and GP2 – now the successful Formula 2 series – and then designing a brand-new chassis for the Formula E series, and he was the founder of the Spark Racing Technology team that still supplies to that championship now. Vasseur has bounced around a bit in his time since joining Renault, moving to the Sauber team in 2017, and was soon promoted to CEO of Sauber Motorsport AG, who then forged a partnership with a giant from racing past, Italian outfit Alfa Romeo. This team was now fully under the stewardship of the Frenchman; still acting as team principal, he is hands-on as well as being the managing director. Racing is what matters most though, and at his level you have to take the rough with the smooth, and with the team struggling to generate points, let alone push for anywhere near a podium finish, tough choices were about to be made.

Thankfully, one decision was pre-empted, with former champion and ever-popular Finnish driver Kimi Raikkonen announcing that the 2021 season would be his last, so his farewell tour was coming to an end at the time of year when new driver contract rumours start to surface, and more often than not, and with the driver pool being quite limited, those rumours often turn into the worst-kept secrets in motorsport. For three consecutive seasons the Alfa Romeo team had gone with the 'Iceman' Raikkonen and Antonio Giovinazzi partnership, but after bagging a decent points haul of 57 in 2019, they could only manage a combined 21 points over the next two years. And now with the Iceman stepping away, it was crunch time for Vasseur. Giovinazzi was a capable driver, but the Italian was finding consistency in his car an issue, and the car itself was not getting any better without any serious cash injection, something that most teams struggle with, even with multi-millions already being pumped in. As always, if you're not winning, you don't pull in the big sponsors and wealthy backers.

Another reason why this was the perfect time for change is that the new number one driver was the steady hand of Valtteri Bottas, another driver from Finland; this one had helped the Mercedes team to the last five of their consecutive eight World Constructors' titles, so his pedigree was good with ten race wins and 67 podiums finishes heading into 2022. A fresh start was needed for him, after years of being the ultimate team player, and playing second fiddle to Lewis Hamilton. It was, to be fair, a considerable downgrade in machinery, but this was a new generation of car for everybody, so with his experience he would be aiming to get everything he could out of his new drive. It was a win–win for Vasseur, gaining the huge talent to fill the void of the other one that had left his paddock, and the sport. 'We always kept a very good relationship,' he explained, as they had known each other since the Finn's Junior race days, 'and very early into the season we were in the same hotel, and we discussed it together one evening. I said, "OK, if one day you are looking for a team, Valtteri, I will be there."' Staying true to his word, and Bottas being a loyal man, he remembered this and now hopes the future will be a prosperous one.

But what of the number two car? The decision was made, and the Italian was relieved of his white and scarlet overalls. 'Saying goodbye to a driver is never easy, especially so in the case of Antonio, who has been part of the team for so long,' Vasseur commented on the release. 'As we part ways, we will cherish the memories of the good times and learn lessons from the bad ones, knowing the moments all made us grow together as a team.' Obviously, there's always a flip side to these outcomes and the driver, despite his best efforts on the track, will feel hard done by. Giovinazzi was left angered by the outcome and took to his personal Instagram to convey how he felt. Accompanied by a picture of himself as a toddler sitting in a scaled-down Ferrari, he wrote:

> @f1 is emotion, talent, cars, risk, speed. But when money rules it can be ruthless. I hope to change my mind about this soon. I believe in the surprise of an unexpected result, of big and small victories achieved thanks to one's commitment. If this was my first picture on a F1, the last still has to be taken.

The money he alluded to, that indeed does rule where racing is concerned, was coming in from Asia. 'This is a great opportunity for us as a team, for the company, for the sponsors, for Formula 1 in general to open up a completely new market in China,' Vasseur said after revealing that 22-year-old Zhou Guanyu would be the second driver for Alfa Romeo in the 2022 season. Born and raised in Shanghai, Zhou comes from a wealthy background; his parents, keeping their heads down and wanting the best start for their son, sent him to boarding school; then in 2012 they moved to England, and his talent was nurtured at the Ferrari Driver Academy in his early teenage years. This was around the same time Vasseur was working on the junior circuit, so he had always been able to keep an eye on the impressive youngster. The talent pool is vast at that level, and it always takes something outstanding to rise above the competition, and Zhou had enough about him that he was eventually elevated into the Formula 2 Championship after working at Renault F1 as their test driver. In a season largely dominated by Australian Oscar Piastri, Zhou had a bright start and won two races, the opening round in Bahrain, and then at the midpoint of the season at Silverstone. Staying in contention for the title throughout the eight-race series, he fell away to finish third in the overall standings but had done enough to convince Vasseur and the top brass at Alfa Romeo that he was ready for the big time.

Zhou knows that getting the drive puts the spotlight on him, and he explained in an interview for Italian newspaper *Gazzetta dello Sport*, 'Of course there will always be pressure when you become a

Formula 1 driver, knowing all the world is watching you, watching any mistake you're making. So, you have to try to make as few mistakes as possible and try to talk on track. I think that's the most important part.' Signing for a team with such a lavish racing history wasn't lost on him either, 'Having the people working behind you, I think they really have the [right] spirit and you got to do well too.' Another of the great generation of young drivers, Zhou knows that the learning curve will be steep but he has confidence in his ability, 'My target firstly I think is, you know, to learn as much as possible, especially in the first part of the season, to put my feet into the Formula 1 world and then build up my momentum, build up my experience in this scenario. But in general, I want to finish in the points, not just one time, hopefully more often.' And of course, he will be representing his country in what is a first, 'I dreamt from a young age of climbing as high as I can in a sport that I am passionate about and now the dream has come true. To be the first-ever Chinese driver in Formula 1 is a breakthrough for Chinese motorsport history.'

The money involved in this deal will always be subject to speculation, but early estimates suggested that as much as $30m would be brought in by sponsors from China, which still brings the Swiss-based team under the new spending salary cap rules for the 2022 season. The cap was introduced to help bring some parity on the grid, and stop a monopolisation from the top teams. 'We are focused on the performance of the team and we don't have to hide the fact that the budget is part of the performance, and we are also targeting to get to the cost cap because it's an important step for us,' Vasseur said of the extra income. 'The decision [to bring Zhou in] is crucial for the future of the company. It was not only based on the fact he is Chinese, but it will be a mega-push for the company, for sponsors and I think also for F1 in general. Formula 1 today is a bit tough. If you are not in the top two plus Ferrari, the exposure is very low, and this is probably the best way we will have to move up the classification of exposure.'

It wasn't long before the two new drivers got to work for their new team, as just two days after the Abu Dhabi Grand Prix, and the crazy finish to the season, Pirelli had scheduled two days of testing. The pageantry of the Formula 1 circus had all but gone from the Yas Marina Circuit, but the motorhomes remained, as well as most of the top drivers staying in them, and key staff. The testing was primarily for the new 18-inch tyres, going away from the traditional 13-inch – a radical change considering the technical advances over the last five decades or more that the 13-inch wheels have been used. The change goes alongside the plethora of new regulations that teams had to adhere to for the 2022 season, and now was as good a time as any for Pirelli to test the new rims. It was important to go bigger, as the new designs would be great in straight lines, but need better handling in corners, so the more rubber on the surface the better the grip as you fly around Eau Rouge at Spa, or Monza's Parabolica. The new tyres would give improved purchase during turns, and therefore better racing, something that drivers in particular have been striving for. The rewards are great for those that take more risks on track and, with the reliability that the bigger tyres bring, allows them to be braver and more instinctive on the track.

Pirelli have always been about looks, as well as performance, so even though they were now making bigger tyres for the Formula 1 teams, they needed to stay on-brand. A slimmer profile and less sidewall give them a modern look, and the wheel covers aren't just pleasing to the eye – they have a feature that reduces air turbulence, and that is of course key to the new car designs. They are much stiffer to help that contact on track, and you might think that would mean more degradation, but it's the opposite. This will also help with strategy – more one-stop races will become the norm, and if a driver can push hard on each set, that adds up to more pure racing. The full range of compounds were available to the teams, from the hardest C1, to the softest C5.

Even though the teams were preparing for the new season's regulations, the cars were far from ready, so 'mule' cars were used. This is fairly standard when testing new technology and parts, and in this two-day test all but one of the teams had prepared a mule car, usually using an older chassis modified for the bigger tyres, with the Williams team stating financial reasons as to why they opted not to. The teams had the opportunity to test privately throughout the 2021 season, but Pirelli had arranged this time to be the final chance they, as well as all teams, could collect fresh data.

Alongside the new tyres, it was also a testing time for several of the next generation to showcase their talents and gain valuable experience both on and off the track. The young driver talent on display, apart from the aforementioned Zhou, included New Zealander Liam Lawson; the 20-year-old is part of the Red Bull Junior set-up and would be given the wheel in an AlphaTauri, their sister F1 team, for testing. Lawson had just completed a dual season of racing where he competed in both Formula 2 and the DTM (German Touring Car) series. Nick Yelloly was at the controls of the Aston Martin for part of the session, after another successful stint for the British driver in the ADAC GT Masters, a grand-tourer racing season.

The immensely talented Robert Shwartzman would be taking on two different cars, the Ferrari and Haas; the Russian, aged 22, was hot property and touted to be a Ferrari driver in the future. The Italian outfit also gave some time to their simulation driver, 25-year-old Antonio Fuoco. After a couple of seasons in Formula E, Fuoco had spent more time in Endurance racing. The name Fittipaldi strikes many chords in the world of motorsport and one of the new breed is Pietro, and the Brazilian–American is a highly thought of driver – his association with the American-owned Haas team saw him get some laps with them. McLaren turned to IndyCar prodigy, the exceptional Pato O'Ward from Mexico, allowing him a drive as a reward for winning an IndyCar race for the sister team in that series. In great hope of getting a drive in Formula 1 soon, the 22-year-old was ready to impress.

Perhaps the next in line of future Dutch driving champions was Nyck de Vries; already a champion in the Formula E circuit, he was already on Mercedes' books, and was ready to assume position again for the team. Red Bull Racing were loaded with talent and Estonian Juri Vips was pushing hard for a chance after two wins in Formula 2 in 2021, where he finished in sixth place overall in the standings. Alpine signed possibly the best talent outside of Formula 1, Oscar Piastri, as their reserve driver for 2022. Piastri had won three consecutive titles leading into this new year – the Formula Renault Eurocup was followed up by both the Formula 3 and 2 titles – and even though a backup drive with Alpine was his, he could count himself unlucky that he never had a full drive for the 2022 campaign; any slip-up by anyone on this year's grid could see the Australian, 20, get his chance. American Logan Sargeant is another that many will keep an eye on in the near future, and maybe after another year in Formula 2 he could be better prepped. Nevertheless, Williams had enough faith in him to hand him some time after only being part of their Academy team for three months.

For Pirelli, the two days were a success in terms of overall performance, but the data had to be unravelled before the first major scheduled testing period, which would take place in Barcelona. Head of F1 and racing, Mario Isola, looked back as well as forward in his comments, 'Today marked the final chapter in a development story back in 2019, leading to a completely new range of tyres and compounds for 2022. We saw some graining during the first day on the front tyres that led to a bit of understeer, especially with the softer compounds, which were run most often as they were best suited to this track. We need to keep in mind that mule cars were used and that the goal of this test was to allow the teams a chance to gather data to analyse over the winter. We'll only get a true picture at the start of next year, when the teams will be able to test these tyres with 2022 cars, which will have completely different aerodynamics, different brakes, and wheel rim covers as well.'

Isola went on to explain that so far the teams had expressed that the new cars were around five-tenths of a second slower in simulations than their predecessors, something that will be rectified during proper winter testing, but with a smile he added that Pirelli were already looking beyond the horizon, 'Throughout the course of next year, we have 25 test days scheduled that will allow us to refine the tyres, if necessary, for the following season. So now, all that's left to do is wait to see the new 18-inch tyres in action on the latest cars.' An intriguing little quirk was the use of LED lights that the McLaren team tested over the two days, 'There was an idea to put some LEDs into the wheel covers, to use these wheel covers also for marketing purposes. That means you can display any kind of message. But clearly you have to test them, because the covers are also an element that could unbalance the tyre. It's really important that the tyre is properly balanced, otherwise they start to have vibrations.' Isola continued, 'When you fit this device and the device is working, you can do whatever you want. You can display the position, you can display logos, you can display the lap time in qualifying or something like that. There are many possibilities. You have the technology, so it's easy to programme what you want to display.'

Testing is not always about quick lap times, although as a driver it's always good to put the hammer down on a few laps and post a tidy time up on the board. More importantly it's about the mileage and reliability, and that was key on these two days for Pirelli. The young drivers on track did lay down some important markers, though, and raised some eyebrows. On day one it was Nyck de Vries in his Mercedes who went quickest; in fact he was a good 1.5 seconds clear of the rest and put in a fair shift too with 77 laps, but it was the newest Mercedes driver George Russell, still under contract with Williams, that put in the most miles on the day for the team with 132 laps completed. Liam Lawson, in the AlphaTauri, was second-quickest out of the young drivers' class, with Piastri in the Alpine fractionally slower.

Lawson couldn't contain his excitement any longer when he spoke after his day under Red Bull's wings, 'I was definitely nervous pulling out of the garage for the first time. I tried not to show it, but I definitely felt it. It took me a while to get to full throttle but when I did, I thought "Holy moly, that's a lot of power!" The ability to have the team update me as I'm out on track was really interesting, although you couldn't make a mistake without them knowing! I really didn't want to get out of the car today, it's been amazing to get my first taste of F1.'

The McLaren of Pato O'Ward followed, with Zhou marking his debut in the Alfa Romeo fifth quickest. The session was interrupted three times, keeping the marshals busy, wielding their red flags; on one occasion it was at Turn 14 when the Red Bull driven by Vips clipped the wall. Speaking after the session he said, 'I had a small moment in the afternoon but fortunately everything was okay, and I was back in the car soon after. I've been looking forward to this test for a while now, it is such a privilege to drive a Formula 1 car, even more so a Championship-winning one.' As with other drivers stepping into an F1 car, it took time to adjust, 'It took my brain some time to get used to the speed of the RB16B because the pace is just crazy but then it is like any other car, and you just get used to it and do your job.'

His incident was the sandwich of the trio of stoppages – the first was caused by Lance Stroll when his Aston Martin broke down due to mechanical failure, then late on Logan Sargeant had trouble with his Williams' power unit, but that was after an impressive 92 laps: 'The team did a great job preparing me for today and giving me the confidence to go out there, enjoy it and do the best I could. It's definitely a massive step up from the Formula 2 and Formula 3 cars, the brake performance is much better, and there's a lot more downforce. The stopping power was like nothing I've felt before! The more you drive, the more you learn and the more pace you find.'

Ferrari had a busy day with three drivers all getting decent runs, Shwartzman taking the wheel from Fuoco, with the Russian going faster than Charles Leclerc. After 87 laps, and his last drive of the year, Leclerc was pleased to get a feel for the new rubber, 'It's useful to continue to get an understanding of the new size of tyre, which is bigger than those we used to the end of this season.

'The feeling through the wheel is quite different. The team has acquired plenty of data, which will be useful in preparing the 2022 car, even though I doubt the feeling from this car will be the same as those from next year's one, given that it will be conceptually very different.' Shwartzman had test-driven for Ferrari before; his skills were put to the limit with the current car though, 'I managed to get through the day's work plan with the team despite a few red flags during the session. I've also learned a few new things compared to previous tests, such as start procedures, which was also very positive for me. Overall, I was quite consistent with the race runs and that was one of the main targets. A big thank you to the Scuderia for this opportunity.'

The following day, Haas had the services of Shwartzman, and he put them on top of the time charts with a flying lap of 1 min 25.348s. This saw him half a second clear of Lando Norris's McLaren. The Russian, the only one of the young drivers' pool that was to test on day two, had the distinct advantage of being in a 2021 car, as opposed to the older mule cars that the top drivers were using. Norris finished his day an hour short of the chequered flag, still covering over 100 laps; only Russell ran fewer, and the new Mercedes man was one of only two men that ran on both days, the other being Zhou, who posted 150 laps, only surpassed by Carlos Sainz in the Ferrari. Almost his equal was Pierre Gasly, 149, and Fernando Alonso, 148, in their AlphaTauri and Alpine respectively. The large amount of run time was helped by there being only one red flag on the day; this was caused by Sebastian Vettel, his technical problem stopping the session under the midday sun.

Australian Piastri was having the time of his life, and this was just testing. After winning three titles on the bounce, it was clear that his future lay in the Formula 1 arena, 'When your engineer comes on the radio and says that [Max] Verstappen is three seconds behind you, that's pretty cool,' he beamed. He was also aware of the job at hand, and despite being close to 1.5 seconds down on the Mercedes, the official test driver for Alpine took his new drive for over 130 laps for valuable experience, 'It was very special. The run plan was very mixed, the morning we did quite a few set-up items, which was nice. I feel like I got up to speed quite quickly. It's nice they trust me for that. In the afternoon we did some driver-based stuff, high fuel longer runs and then we ended the day with some qualifying [simulations] as well. It's such a massive step from F2 to F1, in every aspect. You've got a lot more power, and a lot more grip, and a lot more downforce. The amount of grip you have never fails to blow your mind.'

Having mentioned the new world champion, it would be worth a mention that Verstappen finished 25th overall in timing, from the 27 drivers that participated in the tests, and his rival from the enthralling title race Lewis Hamilton was absent as he returned home to England to receive his knighthood at Windsor Castle. Both were still probably nursing sore heads for very different reasons from the final 2021 race just two days prior. It was Hamilton's new team-mate that felt the weirdest after putting the Mercedes mule through its paces, 'It's a strange feeling because I've tested with the team numerous times after races, end of season, and here we go again. Obviously, it's my first time as an official driver for the team. It was a really great day to be back with the guys and learning about the new tyres. It's going to be very different next year, as the cars are going to be drastically changed compared to these current cars. It's always a pleasant experience driving a World Championship-winning car, the 2019 Mercedes, and with these 18-inch Pirellis, which seem to be reacting pretty positively. Let's hope that carries through to next year and see how they react with the new regulations.'

Pirelli left Abu Dhabi happy with the feedback and knew they had secured the faith of the teams up and down the paddock, their future in the sport is locked in. The next generation of drivers coming through the ranks who would feature in another highly competitive Formula 2 Championship had their taste of what could be in their futures. The fire was stoked, none more so than O'Ward, 'I'm going to do absolutely everything I can, and I'm going to push to my absolute maximum to make sure that I leave nothing on the table, because you've got to take it. You've got to try, because if I don't, I will regret it for the rest of my life. In terms of driving and feeling what it's capable of, and feeling its limits, nothing comes close to this. The feeling an IndyCar gives you is crazy. But you get into this, and just the way it's able to do everything so fast and everything is so compressed, it's like a video game. It's unreal. The best experience I've ever had in a race car in my life.'

The year 2021 had been a long, long season. It had its mentally exhausting climax, which saw a new champion crowned. Red Bull had pushed the Mercedes machine to its limit and, despite losing out in the constructors' title, they had helped steer a new driver to the summit. Max Verstappen is at his best behind the wheel of a race car, and even though he was happy to help his team less than 48 hours after the greatest moment of his career, he was equally happy to get some rest, 'It felt good to be back behind the wheel and it was good to get a feel for the new tyres. Everything went smoothly and there were no major shocks around the tyres, which is always positive.' It was time, though, for Super Max to switch off, 'It was a good day today [testing] at the end of a very long but massively rewarding season and now I'm very much looking forward to some time away from the racetrack!'

After breaking the mould, even champions know when to rest.

MERCEDES-AMG PETRONAS

Team Principal – TOTO WOLFF

Drivers:

LEWIS HAMILTON

British 7/1/85

Poles 103

Starts 288

Wins 103

GEORGE RUSSELL

British 15/2/98

Poles 0

Starts 60

Wins 0

RED BULL RACING

Team Principal – CHRISTIAN HORNER

Drivers:

MAX VERSTAPPEN

Dutch 30/9/97

Poles 11

Starts 141

Wins 20

SERGIO PEREZ

Mexican 26/1/90

Poles 0

Starts 213

Wins 2

FERRARI

Team Principal – MATTIA BINOTTO

Drivers:

CHARLES LECLERC

Monegasque 16/10/97

Poles 9

Starts 80

Wins 2

CARLOS SAINZ JNR

Spanish 1/9/94

Poles 0

Starts 141

Wins 0

McLAREN

Team Principal – ZAK BROWN

Drivers:

DANIEL RICCIARDO

Australian 1/7/89

Poles 4

Starts 210

Wins 8

LANDO NORRIS

British 13/11/99

Poles 1

Starts 60

Wins 0

ALPINE

Team Principal – OTMAR SZAFNAUER

Drivers:

FERNANDO ALONSO

Spanish 29/7/81

Poles 22

Starts 336

Wins 32

ESTEBAN OCON

French 17/9/96

Poles 0

Starts 89

Wins 1

SCUDERIA ALPHATAURI

Team Principal – FRANZ TOST

Drivers:

PIERRE GASLY

French 7/2/96

Poles 0

Starts 86

Wins 1

YUKI TSUNODA

Japanese 11/5/00

Poles 0

Starts 21

Wins 0

ASTON MARTIN F1 TEAM

Team Principal – MIKE KRACK

Drivers:

SEBASTIAN VETTEL

German 3/7/97

Poles 57

Starts 280

Wins 53

LANCE STROLL

Canadian 29/10/98

Poles 1

Starts 100

Wins 0

WILLIAMS

Team Principal – JOST CAPITO

Drivers:

ALEX ALBON

British/Thai 23/3/96

Poles 0

Starts 38

Wins 0

NICHOLAS LATIFI

Canadian 29/6/95

Poles 0

Starts 39

Wins 0

ALFA ROMEO RACING ORLEN

Team Principal – FREDERIC VASSEUR

Drivers:

VALTTERI BOTTAS

Finnish 28/8/89

Poles 20

Starts 178

Wins 10

ZHOU GUANYU

Chinese 30/5/91

Poles 0

Starts 0

Wins 0

HAAS F1

Team Principal – GUENTHER STEINER

Drivers:

MICK SCHUMACHER

German 22/3/99

Poles 0

Starts 22

Wins 0

NIKITA MAZEPIN

Russian 2/3/99

Poles 0

Starts 21

Wins 0

Haas were the first team to unveil the new style cars for 2022, and the hard work that had been underway in their new Maranello factory produced the VF-22 design that looked sleek and robust. After a solid year of development, the calculated risk taken by Haas gave a glimpse under the curtain of what the grid will look like. As with all the cars, though, it wouldn't be until the full testing in Barcelona in late February that any true reveal would be noticeable from all the constructors, something that team principal Guenther Steiner was quick to establish to the adequate media at the car's launch. 'It will be a little bit different, obviously. It's a stage of development, and we don't want to define that. Between the test and the first race, we will not have a lot of changes planned for the moment.' As always at these lavish events it's more about looking good, and promoting yourselves, and keeping your cards as firmly to your chest as possible. No one dare give away too many secrets too soon.

Steiner was feeling optimistic about the season ahead and wanted to push the team to a mid-table finish, and given a year with no upgrades, the hopes were high for the US-based team: 'Now it's the year where we have to prove that we are on the right track with the drivers.' The team head technical director was able to acknowledge the huge changes that all teams had faced over the last few months, as they got to grips with the new regulations. Simone Resta said, 'It's been one of the biggest changes that I can remember in Formula 1 from a technical point of view. The challenge for Haas was we were really rebuilding the technical structure. So that was a complexity added to the technical complexity of developing the new project.' Complex times indeed. Steiner added, 'I know how hard they worked on it, and the results from the wind tunnel, the improvements they do in each session, that's the only thing I can compare, and that makes me cautiously optimistic.'

The flurry of activity continued as more new cars and bright liveries had the covers taken off for the first time. It is of course an exciting time for fans, and journalists, as they get to see their favourites under the studio lights and the dream of a new season fast approaching, even if this one had a gloomy cloud hanging over it. This didn't put Red Bull off; the boisterous team now had a world champion driver to kit out and so their reveal was hotly anticipated. Instead, though, we got a showcase that flattered to deceive as the new RB18 would be fully wheeled out in testing, but we did get the knowledge that Max Verstappen would be driving a car with number 1 pressed on to it, the first time since 2014. 'We'll need some time to get used to the car,' the new champion said. 'It's not like you just jump in and it's an upgrade from last year. The biggest thing for me is the view in the cockpit. With these huge tyres blocking your view, it's harder to hit an apex in the tight corners.' His principal, Christian Horner, commented that the car would have an ongoing evolution, but that would be a very quick process through the season.

It was Ferrari who pulled the rug from under everyone at their launch with a car that looked every inch the car that the new rule-makers had hoped the constructors could come up with, and more. The F1-75 was designed to win titles, something that the team dined out on in the past. 'Expectations are high because we are Ferrari.' It was that simple for Charles Leclerc. The team had not won a race since the middle of the 2019 season, and you need to go back to 2014 for the last time they had a title-winning driver. Speaking at the launch of their latest title hope, Mattia Binotto said, 'For a long time we have been saying that in 2022, that's our best opportunity to be back to being competitive. I'm not considering failure,' he added, while looking at his new charge with a glow of anticipation. 'We are simply focused on trying our best, raising the level, and have a good start to the season.'

Straightaway the car looked like a contender, with its scooped-out sidepods, to its straighter pointed nose; Carlos Sainz was impressed, 'I hope that we get it right and the car is performing well this year, because the car looks beautiful.'

And so on to testing and three days of long sessions that, although doesn't paint a complete picture as to how cars and drivers will set up for the season-opening race, it does lay the foundation as to where and how they can improve. Instantly a problem was detected that would have many scratching their heads, and some even with their hands covering their faces. Porpoising. The new regulations were enforced to give greater downforce, and therefore enable cars to run closer together and create more racing. What it didn't cater for was the effect that the systems would create in doing so. On the long straights in Barcelona, it was evident that the underfloor workings were too close to the ground, and thus at high speed would create the back end of the car to rise, and fall, giving it this awkward dipping motion that would take on the porpoise movement. For many it was something that wasn't expected and had dramatic, damaging effects, but in the main it was thought that the process of testing was to iron out these issues and that it would not be an ongoing problem. If it weren't eradicated quickly though, it could become a serious safety concern. Not just the stress on the cars, but the drivers.

George Russell was very vocal on the matter, as Mercedes were one team that had suffered from the effects, 'It could be solved with a click of your fingers.' He was referring to a reintroduction of active suspensions, something that was banned back in 1994, as it was seen to aid the drivers too much, and now given the cost cap it would be seen as far too costly to have that back on the menu. 'That could be one for the future but let's see in Bahrain. I'm sure the teams will come up with some smart ideas around this issue,' he said, more in hope than true belief. Despite the tremendous bouncing, the Mercedes pair of aces managed to produce the weekend's quickest times, almost half a second up on their nearest rival.

It was as expected, though: Mercedes, Ferrari and Red Bull impressed the most. Throw in some good times by the McLaren, especially an impressive first day quickest time by Lando Norris, and you had an idea of who would be the contenders. The midfield battle was always going to be intriguing and it was the Aston Martin, AlphaTauri and Alpine teams that would be most happy, and then the surprising Williams outing with Albon and Latifi ending with middle-of-the-pack times. Alfa Romeo were the ones that were most downbeat though, with Zhou ending up in the gravel early on day one and Bottas unable to get in a groove. 'I am confident we can make up the time we lost and be fully ready for the season ahead,' the Finn offered after a tough session. The most confusing aspect of the porpoising effect was that nothing was being picked up in the simulations; it was literally when the cars hit the track. Back in the Ferrari camp they were also ponderous despite having thrashed out the most laps between the two drivers, 439 in total; they were some way off the pace and maybe had the worst case of porpoising. Binotto knew work had to be done, from all the teams, 'The ones that will get there sooner will have an advantage at the start of the season.'

It all got very, very Masi

They say time is a great healer, but whoever 'they' are clearly hasn't moved in the circles of Formula 1. Almost three months after the Abu Dhabi Grand Prix, the final race of the 2021 season, and less than three weeks before the start of the new one, the pot that had been stirring and simmering finally boiled over.

Masi had come a long way in his career in a relatively short space of time. Born in 1978 in the suburbs of Sydney, Australia, he first took on race director duties in the Formula 2 and 3 series in 2018 after earning good praise during his time monitoring races in the Supercars touring cars circuits, and also rallying. Under the watchful gaze of Charlie Whiting, he earned a chance to be deputy race director under the excellent Whiting in 2019. However, on the eve of the 2019 season, literally less than a handful of days before the Australian Grand Prix in Adelaide, Whiting sadly passed away. It was a body blow to the sport, as he had been instrumental in the way teams performed in terms of respect to race officials, in what can always be high-tension moments. He was the calm in the storm of a race weekend. Not just a race official, he was a pioneer in the safety of the sport, with several drivers thanking his revolutionary halo system for saving their lives. It was seen as awkward-looking but when the car rolled over, or had another go over the top of it, the halo above the driver's head really was their guardian angel.

The unfortunate death meant some seriously big shoes had to be filled and given that Masi was in place as the backup, his role was now elevated to full race director. In the main, races go off without any real interference from the race officials. Of course they are on hand when safety cars, whether full or virtual, are deployed. They make that call through the help of the stewards, but ultimately any major decision would come down to the call of Masi. It wasn't too long before the spotlight would start shining his way. Whether it be cranes on the track, or wet-weather calls, the buck stopped with Masi, and often he had uncomfortable briefings with media as he explained decisions that would seem fairly routine. Maybe it was the shadow of Whiting that loomed over him, and trying to forge his own identity, but when rules and more importantly lives are at stake you should perhaps take the more logical option available. Through 2021 Masi was becoming more prominent during race days.

The communication between drivers and their teams is crucial during a race. From knowing when to take a pit stop, to knowing the distance between a car ahead or behind, the difference between winning and losing a race would often come down to these brief calls over the radio. Teams, though, were also allowed to communicate directly with Masi – not to give orders and instructions as they would to their drivers, but for information about the race itself. This came to a head in Belgium when in extremely wet weather, it was clear the track was in no condition to have high-speed racing on it. But still, maybe with the pressure of the show must go on from sponsors and television companies, Masi set the cars off. This was already after allowing qualifying to happen in awful conditions. The weekend for many should've been written off. The lights, though, did go out, and at slow speed behind a safety car, a race was completed, and points awarded after three processional laps. It was a farce, and one that would set a precedent for the still-wet-behind-the-ears official.

In the penultimate race in Saudi Arabia, Masi had Red Bull principal Christian Horner openly say afterwards that 'F1 misses Charlie Whiting' after several key decisions had everyone scratching their heads. Masi was in contact with Horner and Mercedes team boss Toto Wolff asking them to allow a swap of race position as Max Verstappen had gained a place while off track, and therefore handing an advantage back to title rival Lewis Hamilton. Now obviously heated words will happen during the most heated championship in many years, with no love lost between the teams and their drivers, and just when calm is needed, it seemed that Masi was either reading the rule book wrong, or just simply making up the rules as he went along. This isn't to say that he was incompetent, but rather lost his way when the situation needed him most. Then of course the following week, in Abu Dhabi, the whole of the motorsport world was watching the most compelling season come to its climax.

There was a concern that the two drivers would collide; given their history throughout the season, it was something that could happen, even not intentionally. Masi would be under intense pressure to make sure fair racing was paramount, and that any incident would be addressed loudly and clearly. So confident were Mercedes that something would, or at least could, go wrong, they were said to have their lawyers trackside. This was only adding to the melting pot. History shows that the race went largely without incident, although the gaining an advantage off the track could have been enforced on Hamilton when he did just that in the very early stages, but no call was made by the stewards. Hamilton had been tearing up the calendar after the summer break and was back to his old self, winning at all costs, and winning well. He was in control of this race throughout, pulling out leads when necessary and virtually coasting. Then the Latifi crash, and subsequent safety car, meant that the airwaves lit up.

Red Bull. Mercedes. Both chewing at Masi's ear over rules and instructions, all the while the cars filing around, the laps counting down. Normal race procedure would see all lapped cars unlap themselves under safety car rules, then after one lap racing would resume. With only three laps to go, this call was made, then reversed and only a handful of lapped cars would be able to pass the safety car; this would bring Verstappen up behind Hamilton, and on new soft tyres that he changed when the initial crash occurred. Masi had taken the rules and bent them, for what he said was to allow racing to happen. Of course we all want to see races finish as they should, the chequered flag dropped as the winning car speeds past, not the snake of a safety car parade. So, with this call Masi had made himself a target, one that would last all winter. He did get his racing lap, and Verstappen did pass Hamilton, with no collision. It was one of the most controversial endings to any sporting championship, and it was caused and created by one man, who many would say lost his nerve when it mattered most.

In the weeks leading up to the start of the 2022 season, Masi was metaphorically in the dock, although he did have to answer some serious questions from the FIA. Less than a month before the season was due to begin, Masi got his marching orders following a lengthy investigation into the fiasco in Abu Dhabi. After three seasons as top dog in his area, he was removed from his position with no full statement issued. It didn't really bring an end to the saga as the full investigation report was not released to accompany the news, which led to many thinking the cover-up was still on. The FIA did reveal that changes were to be made in the set-up of race direction to avoid anything similar happening again; one that was most obvious was to cease all team-to-director communications, and any such talk the other way would not be available for broadcast. As entertaining as some of this was, it was not in the sport's interest to disclose this information to its watching audience. 'With this plan, FIA opens the way for a new step forward in F1 refereeing. Without the referees there is no sport,' explained president Mohammed Ben Sulayem. 'Respect and support of the referees is in the essence of the FIA.'

The announcement of Masi's departure did little to soften the blow dealt by the race director's decision for Lewis Hamilton, who was a mere lap away from his record-breaking eighth world title. 'This first announcement is perhaps a first step of that,' he said, after saying he had lost some faith in the system. 'We have to see actual action and I think it will take a bit of time.' Two new race directors were appointed, and would share duties throughout the 2022 campaign: Eduardo Freitas, with 20 years under his belt as race director with almost a decade in the World Endurance Series, and Niels Wittich, who has experience in the position with the DTM (German Touring Cars) series.

War. What is it good for?

When Russia invaded Ukraine on the morning of 24 February 2022, the world immediately slammed on the brakes in a powerful condemnation. There was no swift robust action as in previous wars, as this was a more delicate political situation than previous wars around the world, and certainly would have a more far-reaching impact than wars that were potentially more hastily made. This planned attack, though, was one that was met with resolve, and instead of rolling over and letting their freedom evaporate, the Ukrainians dug deep and showed mighty resilience.

A widely used saying is that sport and politics shouldn't mix, and to a degree that is right, but sometimes it's hard not to involve the two as they are often very similar in the way they are run. The one thing that sport can do, though, is a show of strength and unity, and so sporting governing bodies started to rise up alongside the political ones, with sanctions being imposed. To try and cut off the Kremlin's head, they would need to starve it, as well as arm the defenders as much as they could. The support, by banning Russian athletes and teams, was one that showed solidarity. Of course the forces that were trying to invade through Ukraine would perhaps scoff at such moves, but the impact it has on those that did not care for the invasion and just wished to compete would suffer too, but such is their way that the suffering would largely be done in silence as opposed to standing up against their leader.

This of course would affect Formula 1 too. One race on the calendar, and one team in the paddock, would be hugely affected, and this all just days before the start of the season. The Russian GP was scheduled for 25 September and, after keeping a watchful eye on how the world was reacting to the invasion, the

FIA decided to pull the plug on the race. Taking away a race from the calendar would only be done in extreme circumstances but, given the way the Sochi race was now being viewed by those within the sport with drivers speaking of boycotts, they were left with little choice. The race was first held there in 2014 and President Putin was very instrumental in gaining a foothold on the grid and was present when handing out the gongs on the podium several times. Now, though, the F1 bosses had a relatively simple choice and during the testing weekend made the announcement that the race was scratched with no plan to install another venue in its place at that stage, but was still keen to keep the slated 23 events.

The Haas team was heavily backed and sponsored by Uralkali, a company run by Dmitry Mazepin, whose son Nikita was one of the two drivers. Such was the sponsorship deal, that the cars' livery was the colours of the company, and for all purposes looked like a Russian flag flying around the track. With all the connections and partnerships, there were long discussions in the Haas garages and motorhomes, and a decision was made to sever ties with Uralkali, and team members worked through the night taking off any sign of the company from their place of work. Trucks, awnings and the cars themselves were to have any red, white and blue stripped off. 'We have to sort out all the legal stuff, which I cannot speak about. We made the decision yesterday with our team partners. This is what we're going to do. I need to work on the rest next week,' Guenther Steiner said on the Friday morning, after the temporary team HQ in Barcelona was now pure plain white.

The next week's issue was that of Mazepin Jnr, and his status within the team. It's one thing taking off a sticker from a car, but removing the driver from it, well that could be a different matter. The situation, though, could be taken out of his hands as the FIA were also looking into the bans that were being handed out by the International Olympic Committee (IOC), as they fell under their umbrella a decade earlier, and the IOC had taken the sweeping motion of banning all Russian and Belarusian athletes from their sanctioned events. Of course, if Mazepin was to be banned, it would set a precedent that would see other drivers from the countries also banned from their championships across the world. With this cloud hanging over his head, Mazepin was still allowed to carry out his duties through the weekend in Barcelona and outperformed his team-mate Mick Schumacher.

The decision didn't take long. Haas, in an official statement, stood alongside the world with its condemnation of the invasion and wishing for its peaceful conclusion. For Nikita Mazepin, his own private world had been turned upside down too. The decision to invade Ukraine was affecting more than those in that country, the personal feeling was now running amongst those that worked under the Russian flag, and the young driver took to social media to air his frustration and say that his own feelings were being ignored in the process. 'There has been no legal reason that could enable the team to terminate my contract on legal terms,' he said. This came after the FIA had suggested that the drivers affected could still race but it would be under the FIA flag, and not that of their own country, but they would have to make a commitment to be neutral from politics. This was against the policies that other sports governing bodies were taking, and even Motorsport UK went ahead with a full ban, which meant that even if Mazepin decided to race under the new FIA compliance rule, he wouldn't be able to race in the British GP.

The axe falling on Mazepin's seat meant that a new driver had to be sought with just two weeks until lights out in Bahrain. Antonio Giovinazzi was hotly tipped, after being dropped by Alfa Romeo at the end of the 2021 season; he still had significant ties with Ferrari. And any thoughts that the removal of Uralkali sponsorship would cast doubt on the team's future were quickly squashed by owner Gene Haas, 'Haas has always been the major primary sponsor, I don't know why people said it was a Russian team. We're good, we're fine. We'd like more money, of course, but we're fine. This just gives us a bigger negative number.'

Out of left field the answer came, and Haas had their replacement driver. Kevin Magnussen signed a multi-year deal. 'Walking back into the paddock, I feel like I never left,' he said with a wry grin. He had raced with the team before, between 2017 and 2020, so was no stranger, and that helped when he was being convinced to return. Of course, hearing Steiner on the end of a phone call wasn't something he was expecting, but he welcomed it and on the face of it didn't need much talking to about the prospect of returning to F1. 'It shows life is full of surprises, and this was certainly one of those big ones.' The move by Haas to recruit K-Mag was a deliberate one to bring some much-needed experience; after a year out of full car development, Steiner was pleased to get a more knowledgeable head in the cockpit. 'We have only got a week before the first race. He knows the team, he's well respected, he knows his way around. At the time [of calling] I didn't know if he was available or if he wanted to drive.' Magnussen had just signed contracts to race for Peugeot and be part of their Le Mans Hypercar in the World Endurance Championship. 'He had contracts in place, and I didn't know the details, but after that it went pretty smooth.'

SECTOR ONE

RELIABILITY AND REVIVAL

GULF AIR BAHRAIN GRAND PRIX
Bahrain International Circuit
57 laps – 3.363 miles/5.412km

The time for all the talk was over.

The shutters in the pit lane rolled open.

This was it: the main event and the start of the new era, an era that promised more exciting races, and further parity amongst the drivers and teams. First stop, 57 laps of the 15-turn circuit in Bahrain. By the time those same shutters closed, and everyone packed up and set off for Saudi Arabia, the usual names were on everyone's lips. Red Bull, Mercedes and Ferrari, although which order you put them in, in terms of talking points, was an opinion.

Ferrari scored an unlikely 1-2 to start the year on an incredible high. So much so that this was not only a new era for Formula 1 but, as Carlos Sainz proclaimed, 'Ferrari is back, and it is properly back!' It was the exuberance of the Spaniard who worked tirelessly over the weekend to ensure his position on the podium. He did not win the race – that award went to his team-mate Charles Leclerc who was all but dominant and excelled in his racing with Max Verstappen. The newly crowned world champion was at his best and was battling his car as well as the other racers, and would eventually succumb to a dramatic late retirement, which some saw as karma for the events a few short weeks previous in the last race weekend. Leclerc was calmness personified, however, and won the race from pole position, even though that was a struggle by his own admission as he made a couple of errors, but the straight-line speed of the Ferrari was a surprise to all and carried him to the front of the pack.

The opening corner, as in most Grands Prix, was crucial as it was Max who was often the most aggressive in these situations. As the two raced to the first right-hander of the season, Leclerc held his nerve, and the racing line. With Sainz tucked neatly behind waiting for any errors, he held off the charging Mercedes of Lewis Hamilton, with Sergio Perez slipping back at the start and allowing the Haas of Kevin Magnussen through. If the opening corners and laps were a precedent to the rest of the season, then the switch in tech and machinery had looked to have paid off. Ferrari had opted to run their cars on soft tyres to start the race, but Leclerc was on a fresh set, with his colleague on used ones. This proved significant early on as Charles was running quicker by a significant margin. Max was free to race with him and for a time did so, but it soon become apparent that his new RB18 had issues. Brake issues.

With overheating a problem, the Dutch driver was being told by his race engineer to lift off and coast. Verstappen, of course, was not a happy man, and an earlier than planned pit stop to try and alleviate the problem was far from ideal. Soon after, though, the arrears on the track was reduced and, after Leclerc made his first stop, the race was back on. These two drivers were known for their wheel-to-wheel racing and when a call came too late from Max's team to once again ease off, he attacked his rival, and took the lead, but Leclerc was not to relinquish his fine start so easily and fought back with a great overtaking move around the outside of the Red Bull. Breathless stuff.

This was exactly what the fans wanted after the winter months of bickering and blame. Racing at its highest level. Max was still fighting his brakes, and in fact this was now intolerable as he called down his radio, 'It's really impossible to race like this with these brakes.' The car was correcting itself, with help from his team working feverishly on the pit wall, but his lap times meant he was some distance behind the scarlet car ahead of him, with understeer also creating a problem. The Red Bull was called in again. Followed by a counteracting Ferrari. Leclerc held his lead, and with Verstappen itching to get after the lead car, there was more frustration as he was being told to ease his new set of medium tyres in. The world champion is known for speaking his mind quite clearly, especially in the heat of race battle, his clear and obvious frustration getting the better of him again, 'This is now two times that I take it easy on the out-lap. I'm never, ever doing that again!'

Gianpiero Lambiase had heard it all before, and tirades like this were water off a duck's back. To any other person it would seem personal but when you have the driver–engineer relationship that has won multiple races, and combined to win the drivers' championship, you can let things slide. The advice is always clear, and a huge part of winning races was to listen to that advice, no matter how much the urge to race without barriers. The problem on the overheating was that the rear set was not reacting very well to the harsh Bahrain track surface, and the balance to the front set meant that easing off was imperative. This did not lead to hunting down the car in front, which was any race driver's instinct. Verstappen was now in the mindset of settling in and driving a race which would see him on the podium, but not with a race win. Then, just as in late December, there was drama.

A safety car on lap 46.

Pierre Gasly's AlphaTauri had engine trouble, which caused his car to flame up dramatically, causing the safety car, 'The whole car just switched off outside of Turn 1, and then I started to smell the burning,' the Frenchman said after the race. This time it made sense for Leclerc to come in and cover off the switch Verstappen had made to the used soft tyre. As racing got back underway Verstappen had a new problem; for him, this really was turning into a race to forget. Reporting an issue of heavy steering, he would evaluate this by fiercely waggling his wheel on long straights, with a feeling that something was stuck. The 'stuck' feeling was in fact a broken feeling as it was later established that a track rod had been damaged during a pit stop. It took five laps to clear the stricken Gasly car, and as racing was close to resuming, Max would test the Ferrari drivers' nerve by edging close to his front wheel, something that was frowned upon at the tail end of the 2021 season. As the cars leapt in the straight, Leclerc was quicker on the pedal and raced clear again; this left the Red Bull vulnerable to the now-bunched-up pack, and the other red car of Sainz. There was more colourful language from Verstappen as he yelled about a potential battery problem. His team could not see any issue. But on track it was evident as Sainz passed with ease and now the podium seemed very distant. Then it was non-existent as his car cut out completely and he drifted off the track, and off the lap charts. The champion would score no points in the opening of his title defence.

The sudden departure from the track had everyone giddy with excitement, for varying reasons. Now the second Red Bull, the charge of Perez, ran in third. With the Ferraris in control of the race, the Mexican had the job of scoring decent points for the team. After a bad start he had fought his way quietly, as he often does, to challenge the lead trio. Where the front two were racing each other, Perez had been locked in his own battle with Sainz. The two were matched well for the most part as Mercedes were way off the pace, with Hamilton being the only real threat to the lead places in the early part of the race. This was down to a strategy gamble which did not pay off; by using a combination of hard and medium tyres, they were the best of the midfield rather than the accustomed run for the race win. It was only after the safety car that Hamilton was on the soft tyre and matching Perez ahead of him. A race that had its fair share of drama and high-level racing had one more twist. The penultimate lap saw Perez's Red Bull give up under him in a similar manner to his team-mate. He had been complaining of power loss for a few laps, and when it finally happened, he had already committed to taking a corner, therefore locking up his rear tyres and sending him spinning dramatically across the track. Jinking quickly to avoid a collision, Hamilton came through and was able to take the last spot on the podium. It did not make up for the Abu Dhabi incident, but on this day the racing gods had a mischievous smile on their faces.

The unexpected, but obviously welcome, 1-2 to start the season was greeted by a beaming team principal Mattia Binotto, 'It's a good starting point no doubt. We were not expecting the 1-2 or were even hoping for it. Charles did a fantastic race, and Carlos as well.' Whereas Christian Horner over at Red Bull could only lick his wounds and ponder where it went wrong, with a full investigation already underway with the next race just days away: 'It looks suspiciously like the failures are relating to each other. The symptoms looked very similar. We know the fuel was in there.' The latter comment came after it was first feared that it was a fuel pump problem. As for the Silver Arrows, it was a day that had salvaged something from nothing. 'It was a lot better than it had been,' Hamilton said, after picking up decent points after a conflicting day, and the porpoising issue was one that was confusing and painful. 'Through testing it was a killer. It's a long race to be bouncing up and down.'

It was a great weekend for Kevin Magnussen and Haas; in fact, it was a dream according to Guenther Steiner. The much-loved team principal had scrambled to acquire the services of K-Mag just days before the season started after the team had expelled Nikita Mazepin due to the ongoing war in Ukraine – the Russian driver and a main sponsor falling foul of the response to the invasion. It was something in the air as the Haas car was fired up with a Ferrari power unit and after qualifying seventh it ran handily all day, and the late retirements of the two Red Bulls elevated the final place to fifth. Valtteri Bottas did not look out of place in his Alfa Romeo as he grabbed sixth place, and his rookie team-mate Zhou Guanyu scored a super tenth to gain the last point available. 'I am so happy, I am speechless. My biggest dream was to race in F1, then to score points and tonight we did both,' a jubilant Zhou told reporters.

It was, though, a day to forget for the McLaren team. They had tested well before the season and with two undoubted talented drivers were optimistic coming into the season opener. They may not have the set-up to outrun the three favoured cars on the grid but the whole weekend was a case of back to the drawing board, 'I'm sure it looks just as bad as it felt. It's just where we are, quite simply. We just have to get a little bit used to it now,' a deflated Lando Norris said after the race in the media scrum. It wasn't any better for Daniel Ricciardo as he failed to get out of the first round of qualifying, then was running last for a brief time, 'There's a lot to try and understand. I think we lack just probably a little bit of downforce and that's really the key. We're just lacking overall grip.' Even though he did not finish in the points it was a weekend of positives for Alex Albon as he returned to racing with Williams. Starting in 14th, he gained one place by the race end, and at one stage threatened to score points: 'We had a good start to the race and were even further up and you could even say a little bit out of place than what we were expecting.' Running in midfield is probably the best place to find out if following and overtaking is easier under the new rules. Albon offered this up in his post-race comments, 'When you get very close it gets similar to previous years, so within half a second. But I was pleasantly surprised by it.'

PIT STOP 1

It was reported that some races would lose slots in the calendar. A warning that with new venues like Qatar and Las Vegas on the horizon, more established venues could well miss out. There is an agreement set in place, under the terms of the Concorde Agreement, that no more than 25 races will form part of the F1 season. But F1 CEO Stefano Domenicali warned that a rotation could be put in place, or some would just be left out. 'There are some promoters who have expiring agreements, and probably some of the current Grands Prix will no longer be part of the calendar,' he said. Historic circuits and locations could be under threat, such as Belgium and Monaco.

PIT STOP 2

In Formula 2, the season also started in Bahrain, and the pack is loaded with talent looking to take the step up into F1. The race was won by Frenchman Theo Pourchaire, racing for the ART Grand Prix team. His victory was by the short margin of 0.9s, ahead of New Zealander Liam Lawson in the Carlin; picking up third place was Juri Vips for Hitech GP a further 0.8s back.

RACE RESULTS

1.	Charles Leclerc	Ferrari	1hr 37m 33.5s
2.	Carlos Sainz Jnr	Ferrari	+5.5s
3.	Lewis Hamilton	Mercedes	+9.6s
4.	George Russell	Mercedes	+11.2s
5.	Kevin Magnussen	Haas	+14.7s
6.	Valtteri Bottas	Alfa Romeo	+16.1s
7.	Esteban Ocon	Alpine	+19.4s
8.	Yuki Tsunoda	AlphaTauri	+20.3s
9.	Fernando Alonso	Alpine	+22.3s
10.	Zhou Guanyu	Alfa Romeo	+23.0s
11.	Mick Schumacher	Haas	+32.5s
12.	Lance Stroll	Aston Martin	+45.8s
13.	Alexander Albon	Williams	+53.9s
14.	Daniel Ricciardo	McLaren	+54.9s
15.	Lando Norris	McLaren	+56.3s
16.	Nicholas Latifi	Williams	+1m 1.7s
17.	Nico Hulkenberg	Aston Martin	+1m 3.8s
18.	Sergio Perez	Red Bull	56 laps - fuel system
19.	Max Verstappen	Red Bull	54 laps - fuel system
20.	Pierre Gasly	AlphaTauri	44 laps - engine

Fastest Lap - Charles Leclerc 1m 34.5s

Drivers' Championship Standings

1. Leclerc	26pts
2. Sainz	18
3. Hamilton	15
4. Russell	12
5. Magnussen	10
6. Bottas	8
7. Ocon	6
8. Tsunoda	4
9. Alonso	2
10. Zhou	1

Constructors' Championship Standings

1. Ferrari	44pts
2. Mercedes	27
3. Haas	10
4. Alfa Romeo	9
5. Alpine	8
6. AlphaTauri	4

STC SAUDI ARABIAN GRAND PRIX
Jeddah Street Circuit
50 laps - 3.830 miles/6.175km

Just as a week before in Bahrain, the main attraction was the battle between the champion Verstappen and the Ferrari of Leclerc. For most of the race it was the Monegasque racer having the upper hand, but overall, there was not much to choose between the two men and their cars. This was pure racing at its finest, done by two great adversaries, with no underlying tension of the year before. The mutual respect was there, along with the tenacity that one comes to expect from an F1 driver.

It did look like Leclerc would have back-to-back wins to open the season, but just as seven days before when the Red Bull had growing pains, it was the turn of the Prancing Horse to throw a shoe. A rear tyre was giving Charles grief and with just five laps to go it caused some serious oversteering. This allowed an already close Verstappen to get the bit firmly between his teeth. The champion did not need a second invitation as Leclerc squirrelled through corners, and took his first win of the year. The Jeddah circuit was one that proved perfect for the new regulations, although far from perfect given the circumstances of the weekend. After much deliberation and consideration after the Houthi attack, the race went ahead. It seemed incredible that a modern race could be jeopardised by falling missiles, but the world landscape is ever-changing. With the deal to stage the event here for ten years, the stakes were high to continue racing, and with that deal amounting to £500m, there was more than driver safety at stake.

It was Sergio Perez who got the upper hand in qualifying, ahead of the previous week's pole-sitter Leclerc. This was the first pole of his career, and was a surprise to him, and most of the paddock. After over 200 race starts, it was long overdue. Ferrari had once again looked fast in the practice sessions, but soft tyres in the last run would not be enough and Perez clocked in a great last lap. 'If I can get pole here, I can get pole anywhere!' he said, referring to the level of risk with the high walls and blind corners. Unfortunately, the session was backed up by close to an hour after a horrible crash involving Mick Schumacher's Haas in the second qualifying run. He skipped over a kerb and collided heavily with the wall. The car was split in two with the gearbox trailing off at the back. This was a perfect example of the new safety design, although no one ever wants to see it put into practice. Schumacher was taken to hospital, assessed, and released later the same day, and with the car beyond any quick repair, the team decided to withdraw it and run just the one car on race day. This was down to a cost issue more than anything else, as Schumacher had declared himself fit to race and was more annoyed that he did not have the chance to get into Q3 for the first time in his career.

At the start of the race, it was Perez who held the line into the first corner. And as Verstappen took third place from Sainz into corner two, the rest of the pack slithered through unharmed. Perez took advantage of his fast start to gain a healthy lead in the initial stages; his team-mate was bogged down, though, and felt some frustration creeping in as he could not get much from his medium tyres. Perez had opted for the hard boots and was the much happier of the two, but keeping a close rein was Leclerc as he stayed within two seconds of Checo. Then the first strategy call of the day was one of confusion as the Ferrari man was told to pit to overtake, which was quickly reversed. However, with an undercut in mind, Perez made a copybook stop and got new hard tyres on. This was, however, to prove costly as he exited the pit lane behind the Mercedes of George Russell and could not fire up his new rubber quickly to make amends for the lost few hundredths in the pits. Russell was running in fifth so Perez was already cursing his luck, or was it timing – which was about to become even worse as Nicholas Latifi crashed into the wall at

Turn 27, causing at first a virtual then a real safety car. Latifi had been coasting in his Williams but realising he had overcooked it on his way into the corner, his correction caused a lock-up which meant he could not avoid taking his car into the concrete wall.

The subsequent stoppage in racing allowed several cars to pit. This would include the leaders, who all shuffled the pack as they left the slow pit lane. Leclerc emerged first, with Verstappen in second place, and Sainz in third. Sainz was now in a familiar tussle with Perez, who had managed to get ahead of Russell and, as the Ferrari left the pit lane, the two cars narrowly avoided a collision, but the Red Bull was coming in hot and Sainz had to take evasive action which let Perez through. It was the first controversial call of the season, but then it turned out to be no call as there was no reprimand and the places stuck, with the race still under flags. After the race, Sainz would comment on how the situation was 'very strange' and that, 'We created a mess that for me was unnecessary.'

It was not until lap 20 that full racing resumed, and as it was announced that the safety car would be coming in, Verstappen was up to his old tricks as he edged closer to the front wheel of Leclerc. But once more, as in Bahrain, the Ferrari got the jump and screamed away. The two were joined for the middle part of the race by a consistent gap, no one wanting to make a serious move to fight the other. On lap 37, another VSC was deployed, stabilising the lead at just under two seconds. Fernando Alonso, the hapless Daniel Ricciardo, and Valtteri Bottas all had differences with their machinery and left the track. It was a shame for Alonso who was embroiled in a decent battle with the Haas of Kevin Magnussen, but the Alpine suffered power failure and limped out. Ricciardo had his own demons and shortly after team orders that instructed him to let the other papaya-coloured car of Lando Norris pass, he too suffered a failure. This time only four laps were lost, and we could go racing again, with just ten laps to go. Again, the Ferrari was able to twist itself away from the Red Bull; lower downforce at the corners meant better speed and at this moment the Red Bull could not match it, but the straight-line speed was that much faster, keeping him in touch, and within striking distance.

Racing though is not always about speed. It is about active learning and knowing when to gain the best track position, even if that meant conceding leads only to retake them through acceleration out of corners. Leclerc had seemed to master that trick in the first race and was in control again, allowing the faster car the spot to pass, and then swooping back in front. It was more than cat and mouse, these two were far more cunning than Tom and Jerry. Max Verstappen though is more warrior, as well as a fast learner and was not in the mood to be fooled again. There was more than one way to overtake and as the Red Bull had its brakes slammed on into the last corner, and in a mini cloud of smoke, the Ferrari was through but had given the advantage of DRS zone, but so heavy was the braking that Max could not keep up with the scampering Leclerc. This was not going the champion's way and his frustration was starting to simmer again, chewing off his engineer's ear, who came back with a curt reply of his own.

And so, it was on lap 45 that the decisive moment came. Leclerc was again quick through the first sector, but Verstappen reeled him in, and then at Turn 27 the oversteer occurred. Once. Twice. Then again on the last corner. This time the Red Bull was well within DRS, and up the main straight it was a simple overtake. There was some fight in the Ferrari but in the end it had to yield. Gathering himself for one more push Leclerc gained the fastest lap of the race, but then more flags, only yellow in colour but enough to thwart any final heroics. Verstappen was full of praise for his beaten foe, 'I had a good few opportunities, but Charles really played it smart. It was not easy for me to get by. Once I was ahead, it was really four laps flat out to stay ahead because Charles was consistently in my

DRS.' Despite finishing second, Leclerc clearly had a thrilling evening. 'Oh God, I really enjoyed that race!' he claimed over his radio. Sainz trailed home in third to claim another podium place, and the promising start of Perez only resulted in a fourth place ahead of George Russell who maintained his steady start to life at Mercedes, this despite the ongoing porpoising, which for some reason the Mercedes team were finding harder than others to conquer.

It was a tough race day for the Williams team. Their cars assumed their customary positions towards the back of the grid, but neither would have expected not to finish the race. Having said that, Latifi did have his qualifying ended when his rear lost control, causing a nasty shunt. Then during the race, the same happened as the back of the car slid out from under him. Albon was part of the duo that caused the late yellow flags. He attempted to pass Lance Stroll, but a lock-up left him helpless as he went into the left of the Aston Martin, leaving a considerable trail of debris in their wake. The stewards did not go light on this incident and slapped a three-place grid penalty on the Thai driver. Alpine were having a good day; that was until Alonso suffered a power drop-out. They were often racing each other and had to be wary of not costing each other time, and in their scrap with Bottas's Alfa Romeo. The team had to enforce some order to proceedings early on as Alonso had his nose chopped, as early as the fifth lap, by the French driver. The former champion was fired up and only when the team orders intervened did the pair cool down. With Alonso's forced retirement, Ocon now had some freedom to run, and had a fair scrap with Norris's McLaren, the latter still not overly happy with his car, suggesting that, 'We could have been ahead of the Alpines. Maybe it's a bit of us going forward a little bit and they go backwards.' A wry smile emerged.

The Alfa Romeo season had started brightly in Bahrain, and they looked set for a double finish again, until the cooling system shut down Bottas's car. Zhou, who had gained points in his first-ever F1 start a week earlier, had a very mixed day. Starting slow off the line, due to an ongoing clutch fault, he had to climb from last to a fight with the Williams duo and the green-liveried Aston Martins. This was a fair race, but after gaining an advantage to get past Albon, he had a five-second penalty to fulfil. He was lifted in this standstill, and was given another penalty, ultimately dropping out of points contention. The issues of porpoising were well documented, as well as being visual, but the most painful weekend was had by Pierre Gasly who was literally screaming in his car. He was suffering from intestinal pain during the latter stages of the race, and even though he scored points in eighth position it was a rough ride home: 'I don't know what's happened with my intestine, but I was dying inside the car. I was screaming because of pain, and I'm just happy the race is done. It was mainly on the right side, so I need to see the doctor. The last five laps it was just about surviving, and I was just massively in pain.'

PIT STOP 1

It was also race weekend for the F2 circuit and after 27 laps the winner was the MP Motorsport driven by Brazilian Felipe Drugovich, who held on to win by 2.3s from Richard Verschoor in the Trident car. The young Brazilian now led the championship with 45 points from the opening two rounds, with Liam Lawson in second place with 34. Lawson limped out on lap 9 when a wheel came off. The last podium place went to Jehan Daruvala, the Indian racing for Prima team.

PIT STOP 2

Seventeen drivers are confirmed to take part in the new season of the W Series, with five making their first starts. Many of the leading women have retained their grid places from the 2021 season, and the opening round will take place at the new Miami circuit in May. Jamie Chadwick will start as favourite, as she looks to retain her title, and there is hope that Alice Powell could run her close. One driver not coming back is Irina Sidorkova, who has fallen foul of the war in Ukraine and the subsequent ban on Russian competitors in the sport.

RACE RESULTS

1.	Max Verstappen	Red Bull	1hr 24m 19.2s
2.	Charles Leclerc	Ferrari	+0.5s
3.	Carlos Sainz Jnr	Ferrari	+8.0s
4.	Sergio Perez	Red Bull	+10.8s
5.	George Russell	Mercedes	+32.7s
6.	Esteban Ocon	Alpine	+56.0s
7.	Lando Norris	McLaren	+56.1s
8.	Pierre Gasly	AlphaTauri	+1m 2.9s
9.	Kevin Magnussen	Haas	+1m 4.3s
10.	Lewis Hamilton	Mercedes	+1m 13.9s
11.	Zhou Guanyu	Alfa Romeo	+1m 22.2s
12.	Nico Hulkenberg	Haas	+1m 31.7s
13.	Lance Stroll	Aston Martin	-1 lap + 14.5s
14.	Alexander Albon	Williams	47 laps - accident
15.	Valtteri Bottas	Alfa Romeo	36 laps - overheating
16.	Fernando Alonso	Alpine	35 laps - mechanical
17.	Daniel Ricciardo	McLaren	35 laps - mechanical
18.	Nicholas Latifi	Williams	14 laps - accident
19.	Yuki Tsunoda	AlphaTauri	DNS - transmission
20.	Mick Schumacher	Haas	DNS - qualifying accident

Fastest Lap - Max Verstappen 1m 31.6s

Drivers' Championship Standings

1. Leclerc	45pts
2. Sainz	33
3. Verstappen	25
4. Russell	22
5. Hamilton	16
6. Ocon	14
7. Perez	12
8. Magnussen	12
9. Bottas	8
10. Norris	6
11. Tsunoda	4
12. Gasly	4
13. Alonso	2
14. Zhou	1

Constructors' Championship Standings

1. Ferrari	78pts
2. Mercedes	38
3. Red Bull	37
4. Alpine	16
5. Haas	12
6. Alfa Romeo	9
7. AlphaTauri	8
8. McLaren	6

HEINEKEN AUSTRALIAN GRAND PRIX
Albert Park
58 laps - 3.295 miles/5.300km

Back to Melbourne and back to the top step of the podium for Charles Leclerc. The Ferrari team seemed to have the jump on the rest of the grid, and this was being helped by the persistent problem that their closest rivals were having – if it wasn't the constant bouncing on the Mercedes cars, it was the mechanical failures the team from Milton Keynes were suffering from.

Again, the mutual respect both on and off the track came to the fore as Charles and Max would bring the best out of each other during a thrilling qualifying session as well as the race. Qualifying wasn't without its drama as a track alteration drew some moans, and that's before the low setting sun meant visor changes for the main session. Fernando Alonso drew the session to a halt with a big shunt and this meant that Carlos Sainz couldn't complete his flying lap. Verstappen was having trouble with balance, which caused him to be more cautious than usual. The shock wasn't that the Red Bulls were again being outdone by Ferrari, but that of the McLaren of Lando Norris who put his car on the second row, even if it was close to being a full second off the pole-sitter's time.

It was Leclerc, though, that took his early season form and produced a masterclass on this day. It was hard to believe this was only his fourth career win, as he dominated from the green light to chequered flag. Even if the rest of the pack weren't suffering ills, it was clear that both he and his car would've prevailed. The only time he seemed threatened was when Verstappen got the drop on him off the line, but Leclerc's reflexes were only fractionally off, and he made the first corner ahead and that was enough. Behind the pair, Hamilton was quicker into the corner than Perez and stole third place. Things could have got worse for Checo, but Sainz, who was down in ninth on the grid, had a poor getaway and was being challenged by Schumacher, and when the Ferrari tried to round the fast left Turn 9, his hard tyres were not up to it and, as the Spaniard caught the grass, he spun across the asphalt and wound up in the gravel. This called for a safety car, after a brief evaluation under the virtual one, given the proximity of the stricken car, and gave Perez and the rest of the field a brief reprieve. For Sainz it was the end of a troubled weekend which never really got going.

With a new rule being implemented after the tactics of Verstappen to 'lean' on his opponents' cars at restarts, it was time to put it to the test. From now, no drivers would be allowed to put any of their cars' front alongside the rearmost section of the one in front. This was a positive step by the FIA in response to calls of unfair play. This was something that the Red Bull garage were keen to make sure their champion racer adhered to, so a quick reminder was sent over the radio. Leclerc, feeling more at ease with the new rule in place, was soon back up to pace, but visibly his car was suffering perhaps the worst case of porpoising yet; despite this farcical look, he was soon out of DRS range and back into a groove. The restart didn't go the way of Perez, and Hamilton was holding third place. Up ahead, Verstappen was soon getting heavy degradation on his front left, which at one point had him off the track, and on lap 18 it was time to change, and given that his rubber was wearing quickly he went on to the hard set. The Ferrari pace had him streaking ahead, and as such he didn't need to pit until four laps after Verstappen. He was having no problem with tyres; in fact, he would later recall that the tyre set-up was great throughout the entire race. After the leader's change, he was clear by almost seven seconds, but everyone had to slow after another incident meant flags were once more raised around the side of the circuit.

Turn 5 proved fatal on this day for Sebastian Vettel. It is a fast right-hander with next to no room for mistakes with a wall on the exit. With debris across the surface, the pack was slowed for another three laps. This raised a new set of complaints. The safety car is a high-performance Aston Martin Vantage; they do differ sometimes, but this car was causing grief amongst those at the head of the snake. Leclerc was quick on his radio and noted later that because of the car's slow pace he was finding it hard to get any and keep temperatures up in his tyres, something that George Russell also relayed as he compared the slow pace being around five seconds to that of the Mercedes GT Black Series car. Verstappen, being more forthcoming, suggested it was 'a turtle'. The slowness was considered as the cars went to race again at the end of lap 26. Leclerc, aware that Verstappen wasn't going to be pulling alongside him, couldn't get the required grip to pull away as quickly as he did earlier in the race, and with some understeer he went onto the dirty side of the Albert Park surface. This allowed the Red Bull to pull up alongside but, with the short straight acting as a stopper, Leclerc stayed ahead, and by the end of the lap was over a second ahead by the time they came back around. The front of the race was turning into a procession as Leclerc was able to sustain and increase his lead during the middle third of the 58 laps. The race then changed on lap 38.

'I smell some weird fluid.' Never a good thing to hear on a radio call, especially when it is followed with a few expletives. Verstappen was in trouble. Not for his verbal outburst, but his car. Lambiase knew the race was up and sent over a message to stop as close to the fire marshals as possible. With the car smoking and data showing the fuel system had broken, it was another retirement. Red Bull had been aware of an issue and had thought they had countered it before the race start, and put thoughts of not finishing to the back of their minds. Three races in, two DNFs and a points difference against a formidable driver and machine. It was a hole that, although just starting to get big, was far from deep. The team hadn't suffered with severe reliability problems for a long time, and maybe it was good to have the bad luck now, rather than later in the season. As Verstappen climbed out and looked forlornly at his broken car, the race continued around him, albeit slowly for a couple of laps as the RB18 was removed from the track.

Leclerc was even happier now, of course he would be, but he still wanted to maximise his weekend. Ferrari were erring on the side of caution, not wanting anything overly dramatic, and put off their leading man from going for a fastest lap. Remember every point counts. It was only on the last lap, when he got the all-clear, that he posted the quickest lap of the day, thus snagging the extra point. As much as Verstappen was having bad luck, Leclerc's car could have been painted with a four-leaf clover as, just as the fastest lap was being created, Fernando Alonso dipped into the pits and raced out for his own quick lap and was looking to have gained the extra point, but then came the flash of red on the final run around, to steal it away. Three extra points had been gained by Leclerc, something that could prove vital come the final races. The pace they had was a surprise, and something they couldn't take for granted.

With Leclerc the clear and worthy winner, and Verstappen already in the hospitality area, there was a race for second place and valuable points. The intriguing battle of Hamilton and Perez was being fought in the pits as well as on the track, and with both running on a one-stop strategy, it was the seven-time world champion that got his nose in front, due to an overcut; new tyres went on two laps after the Red Bull number two. The window of opportunity was small, though, as the tyres on Perez's car were already lit up and he was able to get past. This was all in the early stages of the race. It was the steady Russell who was proving to be the most consistent driver, behind the superlative Leclerc. Taking advantage of the Vettel incident, he was running in a comfortable third place. Being warned of tyre wear, he had to let Perez through on lap 35. 'I really wanted to push it further. The Red

Bull was just too quick for us,' he would say at the race conclusion.

This led to a predictable finish as the two drivers settled in for the last 20 laps knowing that only a mistake by the leader would alter their podium position. This, though, wasn't ideal for Hamilton as he was now stuck in limbo. Knowing that his bitter rival from last season was out, the opportunity to gain extra points was on the cards. There had been no public announcement over whether the two Brits could race freely, but it was taken out of the older one's hands when his car showed signs of overheating.

Behind the obvious lead six cars was the happy re-emergence of McLaren. They ran well around the fresh surface of Albert Park, and it was great to see a smile back on the face of hometown hero Daniel Ricciardo. Was this just a flash in the pan, though? With the poor start to the season, they would take the fifth and sixth place for Norris and Ricciardo respectively, with open arms, but team principal Andreas Seidl pointed out that this was more likely due to the car being more suited for this track rather than any significant upgrades they brought along. 'The track layout suits our current package. That puts us in a more competitive position. Heads down, let's not get over-excited,' was the message.

The Alpine team had mixed feelings about the race weekend, with Ocon placed seventh but Alonso again ruing some bad luck but able to put in the flyer at the end to almost take the point away from Leclerc. Alonso was having a torrid time in the car, and it got worse in qualifying when, after setting great early pace in Q3, the hydraulics let him down and he had to settle for a mid-grid start. The safety cars thwarted his strategy, 'I'm speechless to be honest. We lost a guaranteed sixth in Saudi. Here we were looking at P6 or P7 before the safety car.' There was a chance of a podium; that is how confident he was in the car's pace, which was shown at the end. Another chance gone.

The safety car incident was caused by Vettel, and he was getting used to a spluttering car, even if Alonso wasn't. Porpoising, a blown engine in practice, and by the time that was fixed only one real lap in qualifying. Then the crash in the first half of the race. 'Once I lost it, there was no chance to come back. I'm sure it will get better, it can't get any worse!' His team-mate at Aston Martin, Lance Stroll, was also left frustrated after multiple penalties over the weekend. 'I don't get it,' he said of the FIA actions against him, a five-second slap on the wrist and a point on his super licence after excessive weaving. 'I'm weaving to try and break the slipstream, not to try and defend, and then they penalise me for it. I don't get it.'

PIT STOP 1

With the Russian GP cancelled as the continued conflict in Ukraine raged on, there was a gap in the calendar still to be filled. Qatar was favoured, and a return to the Losail circuit. There are, however, concerns over the heat in September, and this means that other possibilities come into play – one includes a second race in Singapore. This would mean back-to-back race weekends, with the chance to explore a night race as well as one held at dusk.

PIT STOP 2

Audi and Porsche are very keen to enter the world of Formula 1, but they are also willing to wait and see what the rules will be for their proposed start in 2026. Rules that include new power units will be crucial to their joining. Keeping a close eye on developments is Christian Horner at Red Bull, saying, 'It would be great news for Formula 1' and 'only natural for us to hold discussions'. Any new engine supplier would be courted by top teams.

RACE RESULTS

Pos.	Driver	Team	Time/Result
1.	Charles Leclerc	Ferrari	1hr 27m 46.5s
2.	Sergio Perez	Red Bull	+20.5s
3.	George Russell	Mercedes	+25.5s
4.	Lewis Hamilton	Mercedes	+28.5s
5.	Lando Norris	McLaren	+53.3s
6.	Daniel Ricciardo	McLaren	+53.7s
7.	Esteban Ocon	Alpine	+1m 01.6s
8.	Valtteri Bottas	Alfa Romeo	+1m 08.4s
9.	Pierre Gasly	AlphaTauri	+1m 16.2s
10.	Alexander Albon	Williams	+1m 19.3s
11.	Zhou Guanyu	Alfa Romeo	+1m 21.6s
12.	Lance Stroll	Aston Martin	+1m 28.5s
13.	Mick Schumacher	Haas	-1 lap + 2.2s
14.	Kevin Magnussen	Haas	-1 lap + 3.9s
15.	Yuki Tsunoda	AlphaTauri	-1 lap + 6.3s
16.	Nicholas Latifi	Williams	-1 lap + 10.4s
17.	Fernando Alonso	Alpine	-1 lap + 30.5s
18.	Max Verstappen	Red Bull	38 laps - fuel system
19.	Sebastian Vettel	Aston Martin	22 laps - accident
20.	Carlos Sainz	Ferrari	1 lap - spun off

Fastest Lap - Charles Leclerc 1m 20.2s

Drivers' Championship Standings

1. Leclerc	71pts
2. Russell	37
3. Sainz	33
4. Perez	30
5. Hamilton	28
6. Verstappen	25
7. Ocon	20
8. Norris	16
9. Magnussen	12
10. Bottas	12
11. Ricciardo	8
12. Gasly	6
13. Tsunoda	4
14. Alonso	2
15. Zhou	1
16. Albon	1

Constructors' Championship Standings

1. Ferrari	104pts
2. Mercedes	65
3. Red Bull	55
4. McLaren	24
5. Alpine	22
6. Alfa Romeo	13
7. Haas	12
8. AlphaTauri	10
9. Williams	1

ROLEX EMILIA ROMAGNA IMOLA GRAND PRIX
Autodromo Enzo & Dino Ferrari
53 laps – 3.048 miles/4.906km

After the misdemeanours of the Red Bull season so far, it was only a matter of time before they had a race weekend more fitting of their pedigree. Max Verstappen had two races where his charge had let him down, and was keen to make up for those opportunities lost. Therefore, the season started afresh on this race weekend at Imola. In contrast, the Ferrari red would crack for the first time under the handling of the promising start of Charles Leclerc. For the most part, both teams had set their cars up equally and it looked like another glorious showdown, but the tale of the tape will show a disappointing Sunday for the Italian giants, and one of redemption for what had gone before for the champion and his colleague.

Of course, this was a home race and the *tifosi* were as loud as ever but the rain that had been promised materialised and meant there was more colour in the stands as umbrellas went up. Even more colour was added with the constant yellow flags waving during a hectic qualifying session. This was the first sprint race of the year, so the rules were slightly changed but nonetheless Verstappen was eager to stamp his authority. Upon being informed that there was an incident ahead, he eased off and protected what he had. The session had been tricky with a slick surface playing its part, and as he and Leclerc once more locked horns, he was that little bit braver. Bottas and Norris came off towards the end prompting a red flag and putting a stop to any more improvements in anyone's times. Norris was backing up his strong showing in Melbourne, with a handy third place on the grid, showing his handling in difficult conditions was to be merited.

Sprint races are encouraged to be action packed and full of sweeping overtakes. The question hung then as to why choose Imola for such an event? It was hardly the perfect setting for that, but here we were, and with increased points for the winner and the actual pole for the main race, there was more at stake so just maybe we could have something special. Off the line the impressive qualifying session looked to be in vain as a huge amount of wheelspin caused Verstappen to concede the lead, but no sooner had Leclerc jumped in front, a safety car was deployed due to Gasly and Zhou coming together. A short-lived intermission, and when back up to full speed Leclerc pressed home his advantage and escaped the DRS gap. The home crowd were vociferous as the lead increased steadily over the first half of the race. Two things to note here, though: the soft tyres will soon degrade with too much pressure, and the track had been washed clean of any rubber during the Friday sessions. With a lack of grip and the high speed, the Ferrari was starting to be reeled in.

Verstappen could sense this, and, never one to back down, he started to eat away at the lead, small chunks of time coming off. In the zone, Max chewed his engineer's ear off again as he didn't want the information coming into him. He knew the task at hand. When he eventually caught the lead car, he passed with ease, mainly as Leclerc knew the inevitable would happen and there was no point causing any unnecessary stress on his car, and the fact that Leclerc's soft tyres fell away quickly was a concern. Racing in dry conditions meant that a more natural order was restored. Perez picked up four places from seventh, and Sainz came from tenth to get fourth. The usual suspects of this fledging season would occupy the front two rows.

The rain fell again in the morning before the race, and meant that all the grid had slipped on the intermediate tyres. Given what had happened the day before, this could be the leveller that the home crowd needed to cheer on the Ferraris. This time, though, it was Leclerc who was slowest to react to the green. Second gear, and into fourth, throw in some wheelspin and all of a sudden, he was more backwards than forwards and saw both Perez and

Norris slip past him. Sainz endured an even worse getaway as he dragged awfully, and as he tried to gain traction bumped into Ricciardo as they approached the chicane. Sainz left space, but Ricciardo was over the kerb and the paint was too slick from the rain. Touching the side of Sainz, the Spanish driver could only sit helpless as he spun out. Just as in Australia, his race was done before completing a lap. After the race he was philosophical enough, 'Well, it's very simple, in Australia I was completely at fault. And here, I think I couldn't have done anything more to give Daniel more space.' He was putting on a brave face, but it stung, especially as he had to watch his team-mate winning races and outqualifying him. In the build-up to the race Sainz had signed a new contract that will see him at Ferrari until the end of the 2024 season. There is clearly a lot of faith in the driver, but outings like the past two will test patience in some.

The spin and subsequent tidy-up operation meant the safety car was driven out; it was thought it could be the first of a few, but thankfully this was to be the only time it was sighted. Verstappen. Perez. Norris. Leclerc. That was the order as the race got back underway after just three processional laps, and it didn't take long before third and fourth swapped places, using the wicked slipstream to pass up into Tamburello. It was long enough though for Perez to steal nearly three seconds and Verstappen was even further up the road, and a dry line was now starting to form, which allowed the window for pit stops to open. Perez was first in, then Leclerc, then Verstappen. Many races are won in the pit lane, the crews working long hours getting the stops right, with every hundredth of a second critical. Leclerc lost almost 1.5s standing still as the rear tyres stuck.

With Verstappen running clear, the key battle was for second, but with the lap counter ticking over, Leclerc was making no impact on the second Red Bull. After losing out in the sprint race, Leclerc knew that he had to gamble to gain some precious lost points. Pitting again on lap 47, he went for the softest option on offer but now had to get past lapped cars in his pursuit. It was a bold move, as third place was a practical certainty, when Perez darted in to cover the new tyres. The Ferrari pit wall and Leclerc had worked out the optimum area to gain on the Red Bull, and thought if they could gain time at the Variante Alta, he could swing into the DRS zone and leap past. Lap 53 and this was the moment, having got to within striking distance. The chicane kerb was to be his downfall though. Being overzealous, he went hard and heavy over it, spun and went into the tyre wall. No severe damage was done but any challenge for big points disappeared, and the podium was now gone too. Limping back to the pits and some rapid repairs, he came back on the track in ninth place in an attempt to salvage something from the weekend, although at this point pride was more bruised than the car. 'I tried to push a bit more, and it was too much. It was the mistake that cost me a lot and I'll learn from it,' he told the media afterwards.

In the remaining time he gained three more places, but this was hardly consolation. It showed the first bit of immaturity at this level, the first crack when under pressure. It was a case of putting it behind him as soon as possible but seeing his championship rival win the race just added to the headache. Verstappen would haul in 34 points from the weekend, a huge dent in the championship lead which Leclerc still had, let's not forget that, and at two race wins each there was still enough to be positive about. The weekend, though, was unmistakably Max's, 'We needed a good weekend. I didn't expect it to be like this. The team made the right calls. It might look easy on TV, but we still have to be focused.' Perez remained in second place, and the team scored all but one point short of a maximum across a sprint weekend. 'This has to be one of our best-ever results,' Christian Horner said. 'We attacked the weekend from the word go, and both drivers have been unbelievable.'

Toto Wolff was on the opposite end of 'good race weekends' as he had nothing decent to say about the car. George Russell, though, had a moan, despite an excellent third place, 'This is the first weekend I've truly been struggling with my back.' The continuing porpoising was creating health issues, as well as performance ones, such as 'Chest pains from the severity of the bouncing.' Wolff, however, was looking at the overall performance and how the qualifying result was the worst for a decade. It simply was not good enough for a team so used to being at the top of the tree. Hamilton, ever the optimist, was feeling the pressure, and pain too, but even at this early stage of the year was starting to concede that the W13 just wouldn't be good enough to compete but did add that no one in the team was going to give up on it. Yet.

Lower down the top-ten finishers and Aston Martin finally got some reward for their perseverance and often slice of bad luck so far. Vettel in eighth and Stroll in tenth meant a happier camp. The former champion, who had tasted many a victory, did go so far as to say that his placing was just like that winning feeling. Another to impress was Albon in the Williams, although he came away with no points on the board. His choice to come in first for new medium tyres that would run well kept him ahead of the more favoured Gasly and Hamilton. His dogged defence proved that the decision to come back this year was the right one. One person enjoying his racing was Valtteri Bottas. Being the number one driver at Alfa Romeo meant he felt more responsible but also could relax more away from the spotlight at Mercedes, 'I'm very happy to be in the place where I am at the moment.'

PIT STOP 1

Theo Pourchaire extends his lead at the top of the F2 standings by winning the main race at Imola, and a seventh in the sprint. It was a close finish though with Enzo Fittipaldi finishing just 0.3s behind him for the Charouz Racing System team. The last podium spot went to Ralph Boschung who was just a further 0.4s back. Felipe Drugovich could only finish in tenth spot, and is just two points behind Pourchaire in the standings.

PIT STOP 2

Ross Brawn, managing director of F1, wants to expand the amount of sprint races in 2023 to six. The sprints were first introduced in 2021 and have had a mixed reception. 'I think [the teams] can see the success and I think we didn't know quite where we were last year with the old cars. So I'm optimistic that they'll all see the value in it and what we're giving the fans,' he said.

RACE RESULTS

1.	Max Verstappen	Red Bull	1hr 32m 7.9s
2.	Sergio Perez	Red Bull	+16.5s
3.	Lando Norris	McLaren	+34.8s
4.	George Russell	Mercedes	+42.5s
5.	Valtteri Bottas	Alfa Romeo	+43.1s
6.	Charles Leclerc	Ferrari	+56.0s
7.	Yuki Tsunoda	AlphaTauri	+1m 01.1s
8.	Sebastian Vettel	Aston Martin	+1m 10.8s
9.	Kevin Magnussen	Haas	+1m 15.2s
10.	Lance Stroll	Aston Martin	-1 lap + 9.2s
11.	Alexander Albon	Williams	-1 lap + 13.9s
12.	Pierre Gasly	AlphaTauri	-1 lap + 14.5s
13.	Lewis Hamilton	Mercedes	-1 lap + 15.2s
14.	Esteban Ocon	Alpine	-1 lap + 17.3s
15.	Zhou Guanyu	Alfa Romeo	-1 lap + 23.3s
16.	Nicholas Latifi	Williams	-1 lap + 26.0s
17.	Mick Schumacher	Haas	-1 lap + 43.9s
18.	Daniel Ricciardo	McLaren	-1 lap +1m 02.6s
19.	Fernando Alonso	Alpine	6 laps - accident damage
20.	Carlos Sainz Jnr	Ferrari	0 laps - accident

Fastest Lap – Max Verstappen 1m 18.4s

Sprint Race – 21 laps

1. Verstappen	30m 39.5s
2. Leclerc	+2.9s
3. Perez	+4.7s
4. Sainz	+17.5s
5. Norris	+24.5s
6. Ricciardo	+27.7s
7. Bottas	+28.1s
8. Magnussen	+30.7s
9. Alonso	+32.2s
10. Schumacher	+33.7s
11. Russell	+36.2s
12. Tsunoda	+38.2s
13. Vettel	+40.1s
14. Hamilton	+41.4s
15. Stroll	+42.9s
16. Ocon	+43.5s
17. Gasly	+43.7s
18. Albon	+48.8s
19. Latifi	+52.0s
20. Zhou	0 laps – accident

Drivers' Championship Standings

1. Leclerc	86pts
2. Verstappen	59
3. Perez	54
4. Russell	49
5. Sainz	38
6. Norris	35
7. Hamilton	28
8. Bottas	24
9. Ocon	20

10. Magnussen	15
11. Ricciardo	11
12. Tsunoda	10
13. Gasly	6
14. Vettel	4
15. Alonso	2
16. Zhou	1
17. Albon	1
18. Stroll	1

Constructors' Championship Standings

1. Ferrari	124pts
2. Red Bull	113
3. Mercedes	77
4. McLaren	46
5. Alfa Romeo	25
6. Alpine	22
7. AlphaTauri	16
8. Haas	15
9. Aston Martin	5
10. Williams	1

CRYPTO.COM MIAMI GRAND PRIX
Miami International Aerodrome
56 laps – 3.362 miles/5.411km

The long-awaited debut of the Miami Grand Prix was everything you'd expect it to be. Unless you were in a Ferrari cockpit. If so, you saw another example of how your straight-line speed just wasn't enough to compete with that of the Red Bull. And, of course, if you had waited to see if the Marina with those big yachts in was real or not, you already had your answer when reporters were walking on the fake water as it shone brightly, as it was hot. Very hot. The purpose-built circuit around the Miami Dolphins NFL stadium, aka the Hard Rock Stadium, promised a spectacle and it delivered. Right down to the very end when those on the podium had quizzical looks when asked to adorn Dolphins helmets.

With Ferrari locking out the front row, and the two Red Bulls waiting behind them as the lights turned green, we were on for another classic duel between the two pacesetters in this early phase of the season. After some patching up of the newly laid asphalt that had come loose during free practice, the drama of the closing minutes of Q3 made the anticipation for the race even more fervent. Verstappen was quickest after the first runs in the last session, but the Ferrari was better equipped through the early sections of the circuit and this ultimately was where pole was won. In fact it was the two Ferraris that would battle for the top spot, and when Sainz 'slipped' on the new surface it cost him dearly. Leclerc was able to take a slightly different line coming into that area and beat his team-mate by 0.19s. Verstappen was having some reliability issues which made him settle for third spot.

Leclerc's pole proved advantageous as he started on the side with the most rubber on, so when Sainz got away well he couldn't muscle his way into the lead and had to allow the championship leader into the first corner. Verstappen had also got a clean start and was about to embark on a risky move. With the rubber helping Leclerc, concern for those off the racing line was about to come into play. The fast, sweeping right-hander could be navigated for an overtake, but it would take a brave sole to do so, especially at the start with everyone jockeying for position. The Red Bull was having handling and reliability issues through the weekend, hence the second row spots to start. Verstappen was the one brave enough to see what sticks, literally, on the dirty side of the track. Getting the perfect start was paramount, and as he got off the line he sensed the opportunity and went for it, and as he drew alongside Sainz, he knew he had the line going into the snaky second section and, not for the first time in his career, put his elbows out, held firm and made the Ferrari ease up to concede the place. It was a statement of intent.

Verstappen would later say he was lucky that it worked, and as the opening laps progressed some would argue why would he push his luck, especially given that he had already failed to finish in two races, and another could be costly through his own recklessness. With Sainz effectively removed from the battle, he and Leclerc were free to race once more, and it was a common theme over this first month. Perez was now the object of concern for Sainz, with both number two drivers hoping to feed off any scraps thrown their way by their, so far, superior colleagues. Ferrari had done some tinkering between races in a bid to get some more downforce and help up the pace they were losing to the Red Bull cars. In Miami there were three DRS zones, and they would be of huge importance. In a bid to clear the DRS punch, Leclerc knew his only chance was to outrun his rival in the more twisty part of the track, the first few corners. As he did so it enabled him to steer clear of any immediate threat.

Such was the pace that Leclerc was setting, the medium front tyres were already graining on the Ferrari, and this meant that Verstappen could start to cut into the lead slowly. Instantly he was being told of the front car's predicament, but such was the visible problem Verstappen was already on the case. He was managing his tyres well, and when coming through Turn 17, Leclerc slid, and there was an opening as they raced into the pit straight. Still, though, Leclerc had the pure racing line, and he wasn't going to budge off it; the only way to pass would be to do so with minimal grip. The graining had stopped on the fronts so he was confident that the braking zone would come into play as well. Verstappen had too much power down the straight and had surprisingly too much grip as well, and the Ferrari had to watch him go by, but with the sharp corners coming, he had a chance to hit back. With the lead now in hand, a lot sooner than expected, Verstappen stayed ahead and even pulled away and out of the DRS range, and after only a dozen laps the signs were ominous that the number one car would coast to an easy win.

A change was made with Leclerc putting on hard tyres after 24 laps, but a slow change hampered his progress more and when the race leader came in for fresh hard rubber a couple of laps later and got them up to speed, the gap was nearly eight seconds. As things settled, it was more of the same with the two matching their earlier pace through the different sectors; this wasn't helping the hunter, though, as the gap was staying consistent. The tit-for-tat racing was about to change with an alarming Alonso crash. The

Alpine had made a good start to his race and from the middle of the grid was now racing in seventh. By lap 39, he was not racing at all. In an ambitious move, trying to get past the AlphaTauri of Gasly, he braked far too late and went into the French driver's car, but wrecking his own. He would later take full responsibility for the incident, but now with flags waving Gasly was trying to self-assess his car's damage, which was clearly not terminal but severe enough for him to be in cruise mode. Using runoff zones as the steering was shot, he came back onto the track just as Lando Norris was racing past. The two collided and again the AlphaTauri suffered damage, but not as bad as the McLaren. Norris put the incident down to 'bad luck' but he was sent into a spin with his right rear coming clean off.

Virtual safety car deployed. Full safety car out. Race back to life?

Maybe, but by the time the call was made to get the full safety car into operation, both the front two cars had gone past the pit entry, meaning no fresh tyres for either. Sainz opted to stay out as well – it wasn't worth the gamble as he had already lost time in the pits during his first stop, but was relieved to see that Perez was far down the track due to a power issue, which thankfully for the Mexican wasn't terminal, at least in terms of finishing the race. It was fatal for actually being competitive, however. The power loss was before the safety car, and when that came Perez pitted for new medium tyres. Five laps had passed and the broken McLaren was finally hauled from the track and any remaining debris cleared. The snake of cars was led around with only Perez on fresh boots. Would this be a race changer with just a dozen laps to go?

The perfect launch away from Verstappen saw him clear, but the two were matched again and this was lending itself to a healthy race climax. Building some momentum and sussing out the most obvious place to attempt to retake the lead, Leclerc was biding his time, but the laps were ticking by. Waiting for DRS to be activated after the restart was also an annoyance, as the lead never crept over that magic one second. This was mainly due to the slowness in the Red Bull getting the temperature back up in the hard tyres. Both cars were hitting the chicane hard and losing time to each other; when Max did so, a rare opportunity arose to close the gap and maybe make the move but the lead held and the last window closed. All that was left now was to secure the fastest lap point, and as the Ferrari admitted defeat, the Red Bull got more comfortable and with two laps to go Verstappen claimed the bonus.

It was the first time in the season that the same driver had won consecutive races, but Ferrari were still getting podiums as Sainz drove a sensible race to finish third, although the newer tyres on Perez's car did put him under pressure late on. In his pursuit, though, the rubber was overheating, and this put off any last challenge. With two no-lap finishes in the last two race meetings, the podium was very welcome for the Spanish driver. Keeping up his impressive start to the season was George Russell with another fifth place, the Briton having placed no lower than that in his first handful of races as a Mercedes driver. He was another that was aided by the safety car. The team were still trying to come to terms with the bouncing car, and had brought a few new upgrades to Miami to give them a bit more thinking time to solve the ongoing issue. This didn't help Russell in qualifying as he bowed out in Q2 and was only in 12th at the start. Team-mate Hamilton would qualify and finish in sixth place. With some discussion over the radio about pitting, it was Hamilton that stayed out and allowed Russell to get new tyres which helped him get past the former champion. 'George did well to recover from his position and we got fifth and sixth, which is good points for the team. I was a bit of a sitting duck in our move,' said Hamilton of the pass, 'but George did great, was very fair, and on old tyres there wasn't much I could do.'

There were apologies and explanations after the incident that ended the races of Gasly and Norris, and the AlphaTauri man was left ruing his misfortune, 'We tried to do one more lap to see if we could continue, and the car was too damaged. I could not even stay on the track or turn left anymore. I was trying to turn right to give room, and Norris came and clipped my front left tyre.' Esteban Ocon was an unlikely points scorer after his start from the back of the grid having posted no time in qualifying – this was due to a cracked chassis after a meeting with a wall in Q3. 'There was clearly a mountain to climb. But from the strategy to the radio calls, the tyre management, everything was perfect today,' he said, post-race. 'I have to say a big thank you to the boys, because everything was broken in the car. The seat, the pedal box, the throttle … but we made it.'

PIT STOP 1

Shots were fired by Ferrari across the Red Bull bow, as they were claiming that the team would not be able to keep under the new salary cap levels. They were suggesting that significant upgrades had led to the team winning back-to-back races, but Ferrari had opted not to do anything new to their car so far and had seen their dominant start seep away. The budget is set at $140m, and, if true, they believe the early spending will hurt them down the line. 'It's true that Red Bull have improved their car since the very start of the season. If you look at the last two races, maybe they have got a couple of tenths per lap faster to us. At some stage Red Bull will stop development, otherwise I will not understand how they can do that.'

PIT STOP 2

The W Series got underway in Miami, with two races, and two wins for champion Jamie Chadwick. She needed to get past pole-sitter Nerea Marti in the first race, but she had to wait as the race was stopped after a grid stall by Alice Powell, who then had a spin through Turn 7. Emma Kimilainen was the main challenger to Chadwick, but when running wide allowed her and Marta Garcia through. The Finn, in her eagerness to get back into contention, touched Garcia, causing her own car to spin and eventually run last. Garcia had her own problems with a 10s penalty that demoted her off the podium. The second race of the weekend was more straightforward for Chadwick, but again the drama was caused by the Finn, who in her race with Powell lost the back of her car, and Powell broke her front wing, unable to avoid contact. Despite this, last year's championship runner-up Powell was still on the podium, and actually got second place when Marti was handed a place penalty.

RACE RESULTS

1.	Max Verstappen	Red Bull	1hr 34m 24.2s
2.	Charles Leclerc	Ferrari	+3.7s
3.	Carlos Sainz Jnr	Ferrari	+8.2s
4.	Sergio Perez	Red Bull	+10.6s
5.	George Russell	Mercedes	+18.5s
6.	Lewis Hamilton	Mercedes	+21.3s
7.	Valtteri Bottas	Alfa Romeo	+25.0s
8.	Esteban Ocon	Alpine	+28.3s
9.	Alexander Albon	Williams	+32.3s
10.	Lance Stroll	Aston Martin	+37.0s
11.	Fernando Alonso	Alpine	+37.1s
12.	Yuki Tsunoda	AlphaTauri	+40.1s
13.	Daniel Ricciardo	McLaren	+40.9s
14.	Nicholas Latifi	Williams	+49.9s
15.	Mick Schumacher	Haas	+1m 13.3s
16.	Kevin Magnussen	Haas	56 laps - accident damage
17.	Sebastian Vettel	Aston Martin	54 laps - accident damage
18.	Pierre Gasly	AlphaTauri	45 laps - accident damage
19.	Lando Norris	McLaren	39 laps - accident
20.	Zhou Guanyu	Alfa Romeo	6 laps - water pump

Fastest Lap - Max Verstappen 1m 31.3s

Drivers' Championship Standings

1. Leclerc	104pts
2. Verstappen	85
3. Perez	66
4. Russell	59
5. Sainz	53
6. Hamilton	36
7. Norris	35
8. Bottas	30
9. Ocon	24
10. Magnussen	15
11. Ricciardo	11
12. Tsunoda	10
13. Gasly	6
14. Vettel	4
15. Albon	3
16. Alonso	2
17. Stroll	2
18. Zhou	1

Constructors' Championship Standings

1. Ferrari	157
2. Red Bull	151
3. Mercedes	95
4. McLaren	46
5. Alfa Romeo	31
6. Alpine	26
7. AlphaTauri	16
8. Haas	15
9. Aston Martin	6
10. Williams	3

PIRELLI SPANISH GRAND PRIX
Circuit de Barcelona-Catalunya
66 laps - 2.892 miles/4.654km

Time is a great healer they say. Well, apart from the early fuel system problems, there was not much to heal on the Red Bull cars, just a few kinks to iron out, a small sticking plaster if you will. So time was very much on the side of Max Verstappen, even after seeing two races where he didn't score any points and a Ferrari car that seemed to have excelled beyond even their own garage's dreams. Yet here we were in Spain and the current F1 champion ended the weekend on top of the standings. What is more, the tables were turning with Italy's favourite racing brand having their own series of reliability hiccups.

There has often been talk of how the Spanish GP could be lifted off the calendar and no one would really notice, given its notoriety for processional racing and lack of drama. With the Ferrari cars set up, or at least so far, for a display that would lead to a dominant weekend, the cracks started to appear, as they so often have when it matters most in recent years. Leclerc was having a blistering start to the season and only his own mistake led to him slipping up in Miami. So with redemption on his mind, and an upgraded car, with a new rear and floor to improve its aerodynamics, it all looked good. After some further tinkering to adjust some early offset in pace, Leclerc topped the charts in all three free practice sessions. And then in the Saturday qualifying, he again clocked in with the fastest lap to grab another pole position – it was all very satisfactory. It was not all straightforward in the final session, though, as he flat spotted his tyres after a spin, and then saw Verstappen clock in the fastest time, only to be the first to go under 1m 19s. Then he watched as his rival was flat out before a sudden loss of power forced an aborted attempt to steal away the front grid slot.

As stated though, the Barcelona circuit was not known to showcase overtaking, and maybe the new rules would help in that cause. Cars could follow closely now with the added technicalities, and with the Red Bull car showing obvious more speed again, it was all set for a race between the two leading protagonists. Turn 1 saw Leclerc ahead of Verstappen and start to ease away. Further down, and two corners later, there was contact between Mercedes and Haas cars, and Hamilton cursing his luck limped around to the pits, as did Magnussen, and any hint of an early safety car was avoided. Hamilton, feeling the emptiness of his season so far, was soon calling for his car to be retired, an unlikely call, as his frustration was getting the better of him. The end of lap 3 and the DRS was activated, but the Monegasque driver was clear by over a second already so there was no danger. With Sainz falling back on the grid he wasn't around to challenge Verstappen as some had predicted; instead, George Russell was now in third place, his Mercedes behaving better with some significant new packages introduced to the ailing W13. Sainz had seen his fair share of gravel traps in 2022, and was caught unawares by a huge gust of wind at Turn 4; he floundered off the track and was fortunate to keep rolling, but now was down in the middle of the pack, with Tsunoda taking evasive action to allow racing to continue.

With this fresh information available, gusty weather hard to predict, teams scrambled, but it wasn't enough to stop Verstappen of all people suffering the same fate. The Red Bull spun and collected itself but not until he had slipped behind Russell and Perez. He now had a front-seat view of the drama between the two, as Perez was sniffing around the tail of Russell's car, but the Brit was working hard on defence, and kept calm in the situation. Red Bull were getting antsy on the pit wall and gave their first real instruction of the day, and season, to let Max have a go at passing the Mercedes. Perez was told that the place would be given back if and when necessary further on. The Mexican obliged, playing the good team-mate role. The RB18 then started to play tricks. On the main straight the DRS system failed. It just would not stay open and allow that extra speed. This wasn't a one-off – Q3 was ruined with the same problem and even though it had been 'fixed', it wouldn't be known if it had been until a race situation. Multiple situations in the race were now underway and still everything Verstappen did to try and correct the flapping flap, would prove that it was not fixed at all. This would usually mean the airwaves turning blue, but knowing there wasn't much either the engineer, wall or driver could do, it was just accepted that the temperamental flap would have a mind of its own for the duration of the race.

This all happened and we hadn't even reached a quarter stage of the race. Russell pitted, as did Verstappen, and the race between the two was back on. Something that was obvious from last season when Red Bull and Mercedes were racing – it was much less aggressive. The action was clean with no provocation. Was this a new-found respect, or simply that Hamilton so far had not been in a position to tussle with the champion? Russell was highly thought of as the next British champion racer and, with the two being young, this could be the future for the next decade. So, when Max sliced up the inside of his foe to enter the main straight, it looked like job done, but as the lap ticked over to 25, Russell was not finished and put a squeeze on that made Verstappen pull back and remain in third. Would that have happened a year ago? Who knows? While all this was happening, Leclerc was putting more distance between them both, and Perez in second, now over 15 seconds ahead. Perez went in for new boots, and then Leclerc had a supersonic stop that got him back on the track in the lead by almost seven seconds in front of Russell. There was no sign of the degradation problems that had dogged the Ferrari last time out, and he was able to pull away again. Maybe the race drama had come to an end, and the Spanish crowd would again have to settle in for a siesta in the hot sun.

Lap 27. 'No. No. No! What's happened?!'

Leclerc was in disbelief and anguish as his engine let out an almost sympathetic whine. Bringing the car back around to the pits, he pulled into the garage and that was it. The race win was snatched away. 'I think there's plenty of positive signs other than that,' a sore but philosophical Leclerc said after the race. 'The new package works as expected, our race pace and tyre management was good.' Deep down, though, this would hurt and could prove very costly when all the points are added up at the season end. This, of course, meant a new leader on the track, and for the first time in 2022 it was a Silver Arrows. George Russell was still fending off Max Verstappen, but it did seem inevitable that the Red Bull would pass him. The DRS system was working more often than not now and almost enabled a move into Turn 1, but the Mercedes would not yield. Alternative ways to get ahead were put into action, and an on the fly call was made to change to a three-stopper. New softs went on and Verstappen flew out the pit lane with purpose. With Russell staying out to keep track position, it was now a case of when, not if, the Red Bulls would catch and pass for the lead. Perez swept past first as lap 31 begun, and knowing the game was up Russell pitted, albeit after another six laps. Perez followed him in on the next lap to pass the baton over to Verstappen in the race lead.

When the third and last stop came, the lead had grown to over 15 seconds, and now Perez had to give way again as he was on a two-stop strategy, and with Verstappen on new tyres was considerably quicker with two-thirds of the race completed. They could have held position longer; they weren't to be threatened by Russell again and it would've made good viewing to see how well Perez could've coped with a charging team-mate, but it was made fairly obvious who was the preferred man. 'He is quicker. Let him through,' was the call to Checo. Knowing his place within the team was one thing, accepting it in the heat of battle was another. Graciously, but with feeling, he did as he was instructed. 'That's very unfair, but OK.' The payback that was promised was not forthcoming and that was meant to be for another day. Those looking on knew the score though, and it was only hoped that this wasn't the beginning of a messy feud. With the positions changed, it was decided to make the Perez car equal in terms of pit stops and put new softs on, in a bid to claim the fastest lap point, which he obtained on lap 55.

Up until then, Lewis Hamilton held that point, a rare highlight in his otherwise unhappy form of 2022. His drive was immense after that early call to retire, and even though he had to be cautious not to overheat his engine, he had been running in fourth place until quite late. The Spanish circuit had been kinder to Mercedes, and the poor backs of its drivers. So much so that after the race both were excited that they were headed in the right direction. 'I feel like this is probably the start of our season now. I think we've finally solved our issue.' Maybe it was the jubilation of finishing third that brought out this revelation from Russell. Then again, with the season only six races in, out of the now revised 22, there was reason to be cheerful. Toto Wolff wore a smile for the first time post-race too, calling the weekend 'very encouraging and shows that we've made another step. Can we fight for the championship? Well, we bet we can!' Verstappen would now cruise to his third straight win. This was very ominous. The driver was clearly number one in the team, the orders proving so, as well as number one in the world. It would take something special to knock him off that top spot.

The best of the rest on this day was Valtteri Bottas, who continued his impressive new start at Alfa Romeo. Putting his car in seventh on the grid, he gained one extra spot due to Leclerc's failure to finish. The Alpine cars both scored points after poor qualifying runs, where Ocon was in 12th and Alonso at the back, which was put down to a 'miscommunication' in regards to how much time was left to start the flying lap. The team took this as an opportune time to change the engine and put a line through the weekend. Ocon, though, was close to getting into Q3, where he adhered to the out-lap speed limits where some rivals did not. Curious, but they both made up for it on race day with confident drives.

PIT STOP 1

After the cancellation of the Russian Grand Prix, there had been much deliberation and speculation as to whether a replacement race would go into its place. Qatar was the favoured option by many, but with it being close to the football World Cup, some were opposed. However, it was finally agreed that the season would now remain as a 21-race slate, leaving the weekend of 25 September free. While the F1 chiefs decided not to have a replacement race, the F2 schedule was back up to 14 races when they added France to replace the cancelled Sochi event.

PIT STOP 2

Red Bull had accused Aston Martin of a 'copycat' design of its car and this serious accusation had led to a full FIA investigation. The case of reverse engineering is banned in F1 and, after a quick process, it said it was satisfied with the Aston Martin design and that it had not broken any rules. 'At no stage did we ever receive any data from any team or anyone,' said Andrew Green, technical chief of the team. 'This car was conceived in the middle of last year.' The newly updated car in question was unveiled at the Spanish Grand Prix.

RACE RESULT

1.	Max Verstappen	Red Bull	1hr 37m 20.4s
2.	Sergio Perez	Red Bull	+13.0s
3.	George Russell	Mercedes	+32.9s
4.	Carlos Sainz Jnr	Ferrari	+45.2s
5.	Lewis Hamilton	Mercedes	+54.5s
6.	Valtteri Bottas	Alfa Romeo	+59.9s
7.	Esteban Ocon	Alpine	+1m 15.3s
8.	Lando Norris	McLaren	+1m 23.2s
9.	Fernando Alonso	Alpine	-1 lap + 6.8s
10.	Yuki Tsunoda	AlphaTauri	-1 lap + 10.6s
11.	Sebastian Vettel	Aston Martin	-1 lap + 26.6s
12.	Daniel Ricciardo	McLaren	-1 lap + 39.6s
13.	Pierre Gasly	AlphaTauri	-1 lap + 40.9s
14.	Mick Schumacher	Haas	-1 lap + 43.4s
15.	Lance Stroll	Aston Martin	-1 lap +1m 02.3s
16.	Nicholas Latifi	Williams	-2 laps + 4.4s
17.	Kevin Magnussen	Haas	-2 laps + 12.6s
18.	Alexander Albon	Williams	-2 laps + 55.3s
19.	Zhou Guanyu	Alfa Romeo	28 laps - engine
20.	Charles Leclerc	Ferrari	27 laps - engine

Fastest Lap - Sergio Perez 1m 24.1s

Drivers' Championship Standings

1.	Verstappen	110pts
2.	Leclerc	104
3.	Perez	85
4.	Russell	74
5.	Sainz	65
6.	Hamilton	46
7.	Norris	39
8.	Bottas	38
9.	Ocon	30
10.	Magnussen	15
11.	Ricciardo	11
12.	Tsunoda	11
13.	Gasly	6
14.	Vettel	4
15.	Alonso	4
16.	Albon	3
17.	Stroll	2
18.	Zhou	1

Constructors' Championship Standings

1.	Red Bull	195pts
2.	Ferrari	169
3.	Mercedes	120
4.	McLaren	50
5.	Alfa Romeo	39
6.	Alpine	34
7.	AlphaTauri	17
8.	Haas	15
9.	Aston Martin	6
10.	Williams	3

MONACO GRAND PRIX
Circuit de Monaco
73 laps – 2.075 miles/3.339km

Two outstanding features from this year's glamorous race in the harbour: one – it was wet, very wet; and two, the ultimate team-mate finally emerged from the shadows and won. Oh, and there was a notable third mention to Charles Leclerc, who had suffered in his home race time and again. He actually finished the race, although it was another one he would rather forget. When the rain stopped and everyone had dried off, there was the realisation that Sergio Perez was now statistically the best F1 driver from Mexico and had paid tribute to the man he surpassed, Pedro Rodriguez, by wearing his racing colours on his helmet design over the weekend.

Scuderia Ferrari wrote new headlines, without winning the race, so instead their story was demoted to one of subtext. Red Bull ruled the waves, with Perez's victory, his third career win. Under any normal circumstances the glitz and glamour of Monaco, with its high fashion and parties, would be played out in the dry weather, which would mean that if sitting in pole position, it was your race to lose. What, though, if there was a threat of rain? And if that threat became a reality? Well, for Leclerc who had raced to his fourth top grid spot of the season, it was a nightmare scenario. Leclerc had bossed the qualifying session and had a lock on pole, when the red flags waved to signify the end of the timings. Perez, in his last run effort, slid across the track into the barrier, stuck halfway across the track, the yellows waved, but too late for Sainz, also on his last attempt, and his Ferrari couldn't avoid the sick Red Bull. Verstappen arrived at the scene slower, alerted by the flags but was in a good place to challenge for the pole. 'This is typical Monaco! For fuck's sake!'

There were more eyes checking the weather radar than the circuit, and when the reports of rain were first talked of, it was a minimal risk, but as the cars formed up on the grid the temperature had dropped and the spit-spots of rain were noticeable on the shining chassis of the cars. This turned into a light shower, then a heavy one, and then an organised panic as wet tyres were being loaded onto trolleys and wheeled out adjacent to the cars. This was now a wide-open race for those at the head of the grid. The announcement came of a delayed start just five minutes before the formation lap was due. Furthermore, the start would be behind the safety car. Race-goers and commentators alike were looking to the heavens to see if there was a break in the clouds, but the cover looked gloomy and, with all teams now putting the heavy-duty tread tyres on, it became a waiting game.

The FIA clearly didn't want a repeat of the Belgian GP fiasco of a year before when the race was run, and won, after a long delay and a few wet laps and half points given out for those in the top positions. With a second delay, and a race now put back by just over 15 minutes, the safety car pulled away, towing behind it a stream of high-performance cars that sent up a plume of water in its wake. Visibility is always low when the wet stuff comes down, and it was now raining worse than it had been in the last 20 minutes. It was torrential. Puddles were forming across the track, and the infamous swimming-pool section of the circuit was replicated up and down the narrow streets. It was the easiest red-flag decision to make, and with them hoisted and flown, the race was suspended. Maybe this would be Spa 2021 all over again.

With the pit lane now full of cars so as not to impede any track surface drying, there was an intermittent power loss and this news as well as the weather caused another delay. It wasn't for another 45 minutes that another announcement was sent out that there would only be rolling starts, if we did indeed get a start, as the loss of power had caused the grid lights to go out and no one could be certain that it would all work fine for a standing start. It was starting to look a bit farcical, but, with the rain easing and the track clearing, the race did get started, with the lap count reduced by one to 77, due to the time limit on the race, and the extra formation laps. Over the first few laps, as everything settled down, it was Ferrari 1-2, Red Bull 3-4. Business as usual. Then the first sets of tyre changes began as the rain was starting to be splashed away from the racing line, with intermediate being the preferred option. Some cars had switched onto the inters before the second restart, and with those that hadn't watching their lap times closely, it was starting to make sense to make the change; there was even a shout on the radio from Leclerc that slicks could go on, but surely it was too soon for that.

With the decision to bring Leclerc in late, he would lose track position and was already cursing his luck. He had to follow the Williams of Albon, which held him up, just as he was making the gap between himself and Perez shorter. When Albon slipped off the track, the way forward was unhindered, and the gap had been reduced.

Seeing what had happened with his team-mate, Sainz ducked in and went straight on to the slicks. Ferrari also called Leclerc in but realising Sainz was in too late, tried to abort the decision and the window to double-stack was tiny. The radio message was full of expletives as Leclerc had to slow down to allow Sainz to move away, and compounding his misery was the tyre change, which was almost half a second slower.

It was a case of what could go wrong did go wrong. This was a mess, and Ferrari had some explaining to do after the race, 'We should have called him in earlier. At least a lap early. Or, we should have stayed out and protected the lead on the wets, then straight onto the dries ...' Binotto was sounding confused over what he had let unfold. After all lead cars had changed and were running clear, the Red Bulls would stop once more, but this wouldn't have an effect on their positions, only bunching the line-up; it was Perez from Sainz, and Verstappen from Leclerc. Back-markers and lapped cars were hampering any progress for Sainz in particular, which made the last switch of Perez a comfortable one, and the race was done. The Spaniard had to stay clean after bumping the barriers after a slide.

The top four were now running at a fairly equal pace throughout the rest of the race. Just after the melee of stops before one-third distance, the race was under virtual safety car rules, then a full safety car, after a considerable shunt by the Haas of Mick Schumacher. It was a breathtaking moment that again had many praising the new car safety regulations. Slamming into the Tecpro barriers, specially designed to move with the cars, it held and did its job but in doing so the car broke into two, the back end with gears and transmission clear of the front, but a significant amount of debris was strewn across the track. There was a pause before he signalled he was okay. The barrier itself took longer to repair than the removal of the shattered car. 'It seemed like we were ten centimetres further out. That triggered maybe a wet patch with the front wheel, which then translated into a rear wheel slide. I tried to correct it. It's very unfortunate and very annoying,' the German said, a little shaken post-race.

Another top five finish for Russell. Norris was suffering from the lingering tonsillitis he had during the whole of the previous weekend, but this did not stop him gaining a creditable sixth. These two were more than equal to their more experienced team-mates at this point of the season so it was only right that they squared off around the Monaco streets. Their battle was won in the pits, though, as Russell had his mechanics out one lap earlier and this meant his hard slick tyres were up to race temperature quicker, and this helped him overtake the McLaren speedster as he exited the pit lane and braved the wet side of the track to nip past and stay clear. Hamilton, meanwhile, was left in a midfield skirmish with the two Alpine cars. Alonso, not so long ago a title rival, would sit and frustrate the Mercedes driver for the lion's share of the race. With a compliment to himself and a sly dig at his challenger, Alonso said that it was 'extremely easy' to stay ahead and that it wasn't his problem that Hamilton was airing his frustration. If only he could've passed him as easy as he had Ocon, who had been adjudged to defend too hard and nudged the front wing of number 44, and was subsequently slapped with a five-second penalty. 'They said if it was last year, it would have been a racing incident. This year it is not,' an aggrieved Frenchman said in his interviews after the race.

In a bid to see fair play, and a hint of desperation, Ferrari launched a challenge to the FIA over what it saw as an illegal move by both Red Bulls when they exited the pit lane. The long yellow painted line that acted as a buffer to those coming out, and those racing, looked to have been breached. If successful, it would land each driver a five-second penalty, and change the whole complexion of the race outcome. Neither car, though, had fallen foul of the rules and they would be able to keep the positions acquired. This was a matter of principle, and saw that a precedent had been set the year before when Tsunoda was guilty of the same move.

PIT STOP 1

Talks are underway to make the F1 calendar more regional, and group its races together in a bid to improve the areas of concern surrounding personnel travel, freight movements and of course its own sustainability values and aims. It would suggest that Azerbaijan could be placed with Japan and China in an Asian run. Possibly put Miami with Montreal. Bahrain, Qatar, Abu Dhabi and Saudi Arabia could well form the Middle Eastern corner and maybe the end of the season, given the weather and sponsors. Europe of course has the largest amount of circuits, and would form the body of the calendar still.

PIT STOP 2

The budget cap was making headlines again as it was reported that some teams could miss races due to overspending in the early part of the season. 'I think we need the FIA to address the inflationary issue,' Christian Horner said. 'Probably about seven of the teams need to miss the last four races to come within the cap this year, from the consensus that there has been up and down the paddock.' The increase in freight costs as well as inflation was cause for concern, and that was on top of the ongoing need to fix and make necessary adjustment, on the cars. 'It's the middle of the field that are really struggling, and that could get even worse in the second half of the season.'

RACE RESULTS

1.	Sergio Perez	Red Bull	1hr 56m 30.2s
2.	Carlos Sainz Jnr	Ferrari	+1.1s
3.	Max Verstappen	Red Bull	+1.4s
4.	Charles Leclerc	Ferrari	+2.9s
5.	George Russell	Mercedes	+11.9s
6.	Lando Norris	McLaren	+12.2s
7.	Fernando Alonso	Alpine	+46.3s
8.	Lewis Hamilton	Mercedes	+50.3s
9.	Valtteri Bottas	Alfa Romeo	+52.5s
10.	Sebastian Vettel	Aston Martin	+53.5s
11.	Pierre Gasly	AlphaTauri	+54.2s
12.	Esteban Ocon	Alpine	+55.6s
13.	Daniel Ricciardo	McLaren	+57.6s
14.	Lance Stroll	Aston Martin	+1m 0.8s
15.	Nicholas Latifi	Williams	-1 lap + 10.0s
16.	Zhou Guanyu	Alfa Romeo	-1 lap + 10.5s
17.	Yuki Tsunoda	AlphaTauri	-1 lap + 32.7s
18.	Alexander Albon	Williams	48 laps - bottoming
19.	Mick Schumacher	Haas	24 laps - accident
20.	Kevin Magnussen	Haas	19 laps - power unit

Fastest Lap - Lando Norris 1m 14.6s

Drivers' Championship Standings

1. Verstappen	125pts
2. Leclerc	116
3. Perez	110
4. Russell	84
5. Sainz	83
6. Hamilton	50
7. Norris	48
8. Bottas	40
9. Ocon	30
10. Magnussen	15
11. Ricciardo	11
12. Tsunoda	11
13. Alonso	10
14. Gasly	6
15. Vettel	5
16. Albon	3
17. Stroll	2
18. Zhou	1

Constructors' Championship Standings

1. Red Bull	235pts
2. Ferrari	199
3. Mercedes	134
4. McLaren	59
5. Alfa Romeo	41
6. Alpine	40
7. AlphaTauri	17
8. Haas	15
9. Aston Martin	7
10. Williams	3

Coming to America

WHEN LIBERTY Media acquired the controlling interest of Formula 1 in 2016 for a mere $4.4bn – that's £3.3bn – it was clear that it wasn't just to have a foot in the door to one of the biggest attractions in sport across the world, it was kicking the door down.

It has been evident ever since that numbers watching the drama unfold every other weekend have dramatically increased, both trackside and viewing figures at home. It was already a well-watched event but, when you add in the spectacle that a US-based media firm can offer, it will of course catch the imagination of both types of fans. The new era would see the way races are viewed change so much that we actually feel like we are in the car, helmet cam being the latest innovation that, as former driver Martin Brundle would explain during a race, gives us the closest feel to being in the car without doing so, giving us that glimpse of what it is like to be low down and looking through a letterbox-sized hole as the car pushes you to the limits.

The United States was taking Formula 1 to new markets in the country, and beyond, but first of all they had to convince the motorsport fanatics that craved large oval racing with NASCAR and IndyCar dominating their landscape for so many years. The crossover to the IndyCar Series had been tried by many F1 drivers; it is the closest they will come to being back in the circuit they were used to, or for some it is the perfect learning curve, if you'll forgive the pun, for upcoming drivers, as now they have more street circuits and traditional F1-style tracks on their calendar. So how do you make the sport more attractive to those that may be wary of the new kid on the block, not that it is of course as F1 has been racing in the US for decades, across many styles of track, but to get to know it is to get to the heart of it. With the new era of entertainment being streaming and a 'news now' audience, there was a simple and effective way to get a quick and hard fix, and that was to combine the two.

And so, *Drive to Survive* was born. A fly-on-the-wall documentary-style programme that has thrilled and captivated audiences since it first aired in 2019, following the 2018 season. Now five seasons later, it still has its following but many now see it as a reality TV show rather than the real day-to-day life of the drivers and teams that it set out to be. As with most shows of this type, the narrative is driven by the stories, and if there isn't any then it has a way of playing puppet master to show off certain key players as heroes and villains, and highlighting the drama that perhaps wouldn't be there if a camera weren't thrust in front of someone. It is always good to catch an incident that would otherwise go unnoticed, but for some the novelty is wearing off; however, the trick is the audience switches to the real drama of a race weekend as the show gets aired after the season and will lose its edge after we know how each race plays out, and any proper news story will be scrolled through instantly online, and then in the newsstands the next day.

It has served its purpose, though, for bringing it into the mainstream, and you will now know more about Yuki Tsunoda's eating habits than you could ever have dreamed of. And in doing so you root for him while he's chasing that elusive tenth place and last Championship point on a rainy day in Singapore. That's the impact. You may not get the nuts and bolts, and the smell of oil that other documentaries bring you, but you'll get a close-up of a Christian Horner smirk, and an occasional Guenther Steiner swear word; in fact, more than occasional – a lot of swear words. Heroes and villains.

The United States Grand Prix has been a constant on the F1 calendar since the Championship's beginnings, with unofficial races also being held during the early 1900s. After a couple of races at different venues, the mainstay for a good couple of decades was Watkins Glen. The track was reconfigured a couple of times to ensure safer racing as the cars got faster, and in the main it was the British drivers who excelled there with 11 of the 20 races being won by names such as Graham Hill, Jim Clark and James Hunt. As an official USA Grand Prix, there was a break from 1981–88, and then three races were held around the streets of Phoenix, with Alain Prost, and Ayrton Senna, twice, claiming victories. Then another sabbatical from 1992–99. The lean years were soon forgotten, but the heart of US racing was favoured on the next return as Indianapolis held eight races around the famous speedway that was altered to accommodate the F1 cars; Michael Schumacher claimed a handful of wins during his dominant era. Now the Circuit of the Americas is home to the race, and it proves to be one of the highlights of the year as it is often placed at a pivotal point of the season, leading into the final dramatic month.

During the years that the race wasn't named as a country race, there were still Grands Prix being held in North America, with some of these providing novel and dramatic landscapes. The circuit at Long Beach held races for close to a decade and would claim to be the USA GP West, to differentiate from the one on the East side when they clashed on the calendar. Then we had the Caesars Palace Grand Prix which ran around the large parking lot of the hotel complex in Las Vegas, which was then replaced with the Detroit Grand Prix, a full-on street circuit which hosted half a dozen races. And then the bizarre scenes in 1984 when in Dallas the track started to melt under 41-degree heat, and where Nigel Mansell claimed his first pole position, lead the opening stages, only to fall back, then have his Lotus car dramatically fail under him, only to have the Brit climb out of the car and attempt to push it, only to collapse in complete exhaustion.

Fast forward back to the present day and, now, with the huge influence that *Drive to Survive* has had on the market, and Liberty Media paving the way to explore extra revenue streams, the circus has a new playground. Miami. Another car park to drive around, but a more modern and suitable setting than the Vegas car park. Such is the new increased fandom that when tickets went on sale for this new race, they sold out in less than an hour, and most of the facilities hadn't even been unveiled; it was just assumed it would be a nailed-on must-see event. A few hurdles had to be jumped, but once Liberty has their mind set on something, it does invariably come to life, at least in F1.

With a market that already played home to well-known sporting brands, it was to seek a track that would incorporate those landmarks, and when Stephen Ross, owner of the Miami Dolphins NFL franchise, came forward with a proposition of using the Hard Rock Café Stadium as the centrepiece of the design, everyone involved with getting this green light was suitably excited. With other legal battles starting to flare up, such as local communities' concerns over noise and emissions, and being a densely populated area, the assurances were needed that the Miami Gardens area would not be locked down while F1 was in town. With handshakes made, and risk assessments signed off, a race that was almost six years in the making finally got the go-ahead, and Miami was now on the map for race-goers to try and tick off. While all this was going on, another race in the United States was being drafted up.

When you think of Formula 1, and take away the cars, you may tend to start thinking glamour, such as Monaco, and the money that goes with it. If you combine those two but transport it to America, your first thought should be Vegas, although there is no harbour for luxury yachts, not that that fact stopped Miami with its hardware floor fake marina inside one of its wide turns. Different from the race some four decades before, this was to be held on the strip itself, and with plans to make it a night race, it would be all-encompassing of what a Las Vegas GP should be: big lights, fast cars and money. The deal was struck and as of 2023 the new, and now third race to be held in the USA, will be the penultimate event of the season. We can only imagine the scenes late on a Saturday night if a new world champion is crowned. Place your bets now!

SECTOR TWO

TURNING THE SCREW

AZERBAIJAN GRAND PRIX

Baku City Circuit

51 laps – 3.753 miles/6.006km

A third of the season gone, and it looks like we have a turning point. It is of course still too early to say it's one that will decide the championships, both drivers' and constructors', but a point nonetheless that has meant Ferrari have some serious work to do. The double DNF, with the resulting 1-2 for Red Bull, will have a severe blow not just in the standings, but also in the psyche in the garage. Far from a knockout blow, it was a heavy gut punch, and with Max Verstappen back on top of the podium, with that big boyish grin, it somehow seemed that the light had gone out inside Charles Leclerc.

Six. That was the number of pole positions Leclerc had now secured this season, six from eight races. And on the other two occasions he was still on the front row. It was another example of both man and machine being in tune with each other, and it put a marker down that, despite the last sector of this circuit lending itself to the straight-line power of the Red Bull, the Ferrari could still be competitive. It was touch and go at the end of Q3 as, much as he wanted to celebrate his flying lap, he had to wait nervously for Perez to cross the line. With the predicted nullified straight-line speed gone, Ferrari pulling out some tweaks in the practice sessions, Perez could not go faster and the Monegasque driver had his fourth straight pole.

Surprisingly, it was Perez in second place who was threatening to take the lead into the first corner, as the two ran alongside each other. This wasn't down to a better lift-off from the Mexican, rather the huge wheelspin suffered by Leclerc as he struggled on a very soft surface. In a puff of smoke he finally got the desired grip but it was too late and the Red Bull was ahead. With the champion getting an even better start, he was fortunate not to lose two places into Turn 1, but as the front two raced they managed to keep the number 1 car back. Perez was away, and after Monaco had a renewed confidence; maybe the challenge to Verstappen's title wasn't from outside, but from inside his own ranks. There was that lingering thought in Perez's mind that he was merely a pawn in the long game, and if his team-mate should get past Leclerc early on, then he would be subject to another exchange of position.

Early yellow flags impeded the race, and Verstappen's push for second place which looked on, but the first warning signs of the day for Leclerc were visible as he raced past the Turn 4 escape road. Sainz had pulled over, the victim of a failed hydraulics system. The Spaniard was already having an afternoon to forget as he was way off the front three for pace, and then, again, time was called on his car. The yellows led to a virtual safety car, and a frenzy in the pits as teams shuffled their packs early. One to do so was Leclerc, diving in just in time, hard tyres going on. All fine except he was stuck. In the air. 'Both the front and the rear jack were up for whatever it is. I don't know if they were linked, if the rear was a consequence of the front, it's something we need to look at,' Binotto said after the event. Luckily the Red Bull hadn't countered quickly enough, and Perez blamed a miscommunication. With the Red Bulls sticking to their schedule, they were over ten seconds ahead of the Ferrari, but the data was showing that the hard tyre was reacting well, and running fast. Ahead was more encouragement. Perez was slowing, and as he did was told for the first time not to resist when his team-mate would catch and pass him with the DRS knife through butter. Perez was in no mood to fight given his tyres were off, and so it was the time to switch, just as Leclerc thought he was let down by a slow stop; in fact, it was a bit of a botch job with a wheel gun jamming, and the driver releasing too soon. He came out almost 20 seconds off second place. Then Verstappen came in for a smoother, if not terribly fast, stop, and exited behind Leclerc to the tune of a dozen ticks of the stopwatch.

Turn 16. Lap 19. 'Problem. Problem!' was exclaimed over the radio. It was Leclerc. It was Ferrari. It was a blown engine. Coasting in to the pitlane and coming to a halt outside his garage, the engineers took over and pushed the car into the garage. 'I believe we can win the title still,' he said afterwards, 'but we need to get on top of these things.' And fast, he could've added, as this was now beginning to look like a shambles. The Monaco mess could've been forgiven if the team had bounced back with a good showing in Baku, but now everyone was shaking their heads and looking for answers that weren't forthcoming. The engine was a mix of old and new and mostly the one that had kicked him out of the race in Spain, and with the already permitted three turbos used up for the year, he would have to serve a penalty to have a new one fitted. To win the Championship was of course still on, but with the Red Bull sporting shiny new components and some to spare, it would take more than driver skill to take the title. Binotto would be the one in the firing line. He was the voice of the team and had to offer something to the baying media: 'It's no doubt that when you've got so many reliability problems, there is a concern. Sometimes the problems you may have are not a short fix. So I don't know what will be the strategy that we need to adopt.'

Verstappen was now clear. Any threat was gone, and he just had to keep the car on the road. Ferrari had gone for the day, and Perez would be under orders, surely. Down the track was George Russell, promoted to third now, but with the ongoing porpoising, which hadn't turned the expected corner after Spain, he was not going to appear in his mirrors soon. There was, though, the need to stay vigilant, his race having ended cruelly in 2021 when in control, so keeping things ticking over was essential. There must have been something in the Baku air that Ferrari engines didn't appreciate as the unit that powered the Haas of Kevin Magnussen also blew. His race was going well, and he had elevated himself up to tenth. His car was parked up neatly after the puff of grey-white smoke, but where it was placed was a danger so the virtual safety car was started. This gave the leader the chance to pit again. Then Perez. A stark difference between the two, however, of over two seconds, the pit crew again having trouble with sticky guns. The two would run comfortably to the end, the winner ahead by some 20 seconds. It was Verstappen's 25th career race victory, putting him alongside greats Niki Lauda and Jim Clark. He was fast establishing himself as worthy of being talked about in the same breath as these and others around him in the history books.

Knowing how it feels not finishing races at any time, the champion had some words of comfort for his Ferrari rival after the race, 'I would always say "Shit happens". It happened to me, it happened to many people. Unfortunately, it's happening to Charles. If I was in the same situation, I would also be disappointed, I think that's very normal. But it's how you come out of it. You always look at how to improve things.'

These same words could be said to Mercedes; even though they were finishing races, it was a painful watch. Russell was completing another good race day, if a little sore, his back feeling the side-effects of the bouncing. Lewis Hamilton had finished fourth to haul in good points for the team, but he was in a worse state than his younger team-mate and it was a very slow process lifting himself from his car. The tipping point for their season was near, as it was clear the porpoising was winning the day. The season could not go on in this fashion, or else the drivers would end up being carted away each race. 'He's really bad,' said Toto Wolff about Hamilton's back. 'We've just got to find a solution. I think he is maybe the worst affected from all drivers. You can see it's not muscular anymore. This goes properly into the spine and can have some consequences.'

At last Pierre Gasly had a happy race. It had been a mixed season so far for the AlphaTauri man. Fifth place was a welcome reward for battling hard with Hamilton for the main part of the race. It could have been different if the strategy had been cleaner but the VSCs that came into play and a decision to stay out when others changed tyres late on meant that he couldn't keep pace at the end and settled for a commendable fifth. He was placed in front of Sebastian Vettel's Aston Martin, another driver that had his best finish of the year so far. The Alpine of Esteban Ocon had caused Vettel to go off, and if it wasn't for that, he may have had more points. His start from ninth was clean and gained early places, but his trip down the escape road at Turn 3 to avoid Ocon was costly as Hamilton and Tsunoda slipped by. Gaining a place back due to damage on the front wing of the Japanese driver's car, Vettel settled in for his top-six finish: 'Without that incident [with Ocon], I think I could have battled for fifth position. Nevertheless, this is a great result.'

The papaya McLaren cars had a strange day. Yes, they both finished in the points, but the team orders and different strategies made for an interesting time.

With Norris sporting a medium set to start, and Ricciardo wearing hards, the latter was keen to stay out when the first virtual safety car arrived. Norris stopped and didn't overcut Alonso, which was the plan; this had a knock-on effect as Ricciardo was now stuck behind Gasly who had stopped even sooner, and Hamilton was on the Aussie's tail to then slip past. When Ricciardo eventually came in and put a medium set on, he was comfortably ahead of his team-mate, but with Norris charging with bedded-in rubber, it became a close race between the two, but with both cars behind Alonso.

PIT STOP 1

The South African Grand Prix could be back on, and as early as next season – this according to CEO Stefano Domenicali. The Kyalami circuit would be another piece in the puzzle as bosses look to be truly global. There has not been a South African GP since 1993, but early talks were promising, and Domenicali was keen to get things sorted soon.

PIT STOP 2

The cost cap was still hanging heavy over the F1 paddock. McLaren were now very wary of how they could continue late into the season without any breach of the cap. Team principal Andreas Seidl, when pushed on the subject, admitted, 'For us as a team that was planned to run at the cap at the beginning of the year, with all these unexpected costs that came up, we are at a position where we can't make the cap anymore. I'm still hopeful with all the conversations that are happening at the moment, together with the other teams, with FIA and F1, that we still find the best interests of the sport moving forward.' The talks were asking for an increase in the budget, which some teams were unhappy about. Alpine and Alfa Romeo had spoken quite clearly in their opposition of a raise from the $140m.

RACE RESULTS

	Driver	Team	Result
1.	Max Verstappen	Red Bull	1hr 34.0s
2.	Sergio Perez	Red Bull	+20.8s
3.	George Russell	Mercedes	+45.9s
4.	Lewis Hamilton	Mercedes	+1m 11.6s
5.	Pierre Gasly	AlphaTauri	+1m 17.2s
6.	Sebastian Vettel	Aston Martin	+1m 24.0s
7.	Fernando Alonso	Alpine	+1m 28.5s
8.	Daniel Ricciardo	McLaren	+1m 32.2s
9.	Lando Norris	McLaren	+1m 32.5s
10.	Esteban Ocon	Alpine	+1m 48.1s
11.	Valtteri Bottas	Alfa Romeo	-1 lap + 5.5s
12.	Alexander Albon	Williams	-1 lap + 7.2s
13.	Yuki Tsunoda	AlphaTauri	-1 lap + 8.8s
14.	Mick Schumacher	Haas	-1 lap + 47.4s
15.	Nicholas Latifi	Williams	-1 lap + 1m 45.4s
16.	Lance Stroll	Aston Martin	-5 laps - vibration
17.	Kevin Magnussen	Haas	31 laps - engine
18.	Zhou Guanyu	Alfa Romeo	23 laps - hydraulics
19.	Charles Leclerc	Ferrari	21 laps - power unit
20.	Carlos Sainz Jnr	Ferrari	8 laps - hydraulics

Fastest Lap - Sergio Perez 1m 46.0s

Drivers' Championship Standings

1.	Verstappen	150pts
2.	Perez	129
3.	Leclerc	116
4.	Russell	99
5.	Sainz	83
6.	Hamilton	62
7.	Norris	50
8.	Bottas	40
9.	Ocon	31
10.	Gasly	16
11.	Alonso	16
12.	Magnussen	15
13.	Ricciardo	15
14.	Vettel	13
15.	Tsunoda	11
16.	Albon	3
17.	Stroll	2
18.	Zhou	1

Constructors' Championship Standings

1.	Red Bull	279 pts
2.	Ferrari	199
3.	Mercedes	161
4.	McLaren	65
5.	Alpine	47
6.	Alfa Romeo	41
7.	AlphaTauri	27
8.	Haas	15
9.	Aston Martin	15
10.	Williams	3

CANADIAN GRAND PRIX
Circuit Gilles Villeneuve
70 laps – 2.710 miles/4.361km

It wasn't so much 'O Canada' as it was 'oh Canada' as the Ferrari team were 'oh so close, yet so far' from causing a dramatic win and podium from the back of the grid, for Carlos Sainz and Charles Leclerc, respectively. Sainz would openly declare himself the fastest man on the track in post-race comments, and the facts backed it up. This was a serious upturn in his fortunes given the past month or so. This was the first time F1 had visited Montreal since 2019, and even though the Ferrari cars were fast and ultra-competitive, it was Max Verstappen who again claimed a race win.

There was a wild card at the head of the grid though. It wasn't so much that Verstappen had pole position due to the penalty placed on Leclerc to start from the back, a new power unit being the cause, it was the unfamiliar sight of an Alpine, even if the driver in the cockpit was used to the surroundings. Fernando Alonso. It was a dry and wet Friday and Saturday respectively, which fed into the Alpine team's hands somewhat, or at least for the fast style of Alonso, who took the challenge to Verstappen throughout the session. On wets, but nowhere near as bad as the Monaco race, the early pressure told on the current champion as he took a spin early in Q1 but, as the track dried, the water being sprayed to safe areas of the track, he started to turn the screw. Sainz briefly came into play but ran too hard in the last corner and that cost him time as he bumped over the kerb. Then Alonso came racing through taking all the risks in the first sector, to see it pay off as he charged over the final kerbs and, using all his experience, gained his first front row for a decade.

Given his aggressive style, it made for some good overnight headlines as Alonso would do his utmost to make the first-corner battle a spectacle, even if the man himself was playing it down. It was, though, an anti-climax as Max was clean away from his pole slot and into the corner with not a second thought of what was happening alongside him. Sainz challenged as fourth-placed Hamilton locked up and for those first moments it was positions held. The dogged Alonso held off for a bit longer, but on the third lap, the long back straight was his enemy too; with the DRS enabled, Sainz shot past him but now the gap to the leader was already up over three seconds.

It was all going to plan for Verstappen up front, only to see his tyres start to grain, and then his lead start to be chipped away. One cause of this could've been the cooler air, coupled with a fresher track, as rain had taken a lot of the rubber laid down through the early practice sessions. The same problem was being suffered with other cars, and Sainz was starting to benefit, but he too had some lines appearing on his set of boots.

The race was settling though, and with the teams discussing an earlier-than-expected pit window, the Red Bull of Perez, who was down in 13th at the start, suffered a gearbox failure. It was the end of a bad few days for the Mexican, and he trundled off the track and triggered a virtual safety car. This served as very convenient for the rest of the pack who could make the stop, if needed, for tyres – which Verstappen duly did but, with a call from Sainz to his engineer that his set was fine and that the graining phase had passed, stayed out. Verstappen had fallen back into line behind the VSC train, in third behind Alonso, but soon after the restart was able to catch and pass the Alpine with ease. Alonso would know that his fight was further down the train, and that once the usual suspects started to go by he had to run his own race. Red Bull were obviously now on a two-stop strategy, and somehow would have to get past, extend a lead before changing again, as Sainz was likely on a one-stopper.

Both cars were running consistent times with the Red Bull marginally quicker, not that it was making a dramatic difference. That was until in the same area

Checo had pulled off the track, the Haas car of Mick Schumacher did also. It was another engine failure for the German, who had so often promised on delivering his first-ever points finish, only to have it taken away through bad luck, or bad mistakes. This changed the outlook as Sainz took this opportunity to swerve into the pit lane under the VSC, but with good data showing that the hard tyres his team-mate were on as he charged through the field were holding up; so with a switch to those it looked like the one-stop could still be a possibility.

With Alonso staying out, he was now back in front of Sainz; the two Spaniards were not in the same league pace-wise and the Ferrari again passed with no issue. Now, though, the gap to the lead was close to ten seconds, but again the lead was being slowly worked down, and with just over 40 laps gone, it was down to six seconds. It was now that the Red Bull called the race leader in and put the second set of hard tyres on, and now we could really see the merits of the champion's racing as he had 25 laps to cut a lead of 11 seconds – it was very much race on. This is when the decision had to be made as, if the Ferrari car stayed the distance on this set, it would be a 50-lap run, really on the limit. Estimates from the pit wall suggested that Verstappen would catch the leader with around 10 to 12 laps to go. Both teams were calculating the risk and reward situation as the two drivers continued to press on.

Lap 48 and the strategists were given a brief respite as Tsunoda locked up his new tyres and sent his AlphaTauri clean into the barriers, the front of his car completely ruined, and forcing the real safety car into operation. This happened at almost the same time as the decision to bring Sainz in had been made, prompting some sharp looks from the pit wall. The one-stopper was on, and it would have called for good racing; there was a risk though and now it was a case of we'll never know. Sainz would look back on his second stop as 'a shame' as 'he wouldn't have caught me easy. I was ready to hang it out there until the chequered flag.' With the two cars now together for the restart, it was advantage Verstappen as he leaped away when the safety car was called in, Sainz holding back, and with 16 laps to go it was down to who could get the best performance from their cars while looking after the tyres. Keeping in DRS range was key as well as there would be no activation for three laps. It was here that Red Bull knew that the winning experience their man had could be the difference and with Sainz trying to keep withing striking distance he was fighting the car over the kerbs and through bad lines, and when the DRS was open he was all over the back of the car in front. Verstappen's defence of the lead was golden and Sainz, despite having a handful of windows to pass, just couldn't get enough out of his car, and the final distance between the two when the chequered flag dropped was less than a second.

For six races now Verstappen had visited the top step of the podium. His season looked in tatters early on with two DNFs but he stayed calm in the battle and, while the others were wilting around him, his lead in the Championship was effectively two races worth of points. Leclerc had slipped into third place and he was on a salvage mission after taking the brand-new engine, and his fifth place was very admirable, showing his own class, and that of the Ferrari if it could stay in one piece. Sporting a new rear wing too, he was soon making his way through the back end of the grid. As with any superior car starting from the back, it was a case of timing and patience to get past the slower vehicles, almost a road stop in some cases, and by the time Perez had fallen out of the race, he was in 13th, when maybe hoping to be a little higher. It was the DRS train which came into effect in the middle part of the race that hampered him as well as threading through equally matched cars, which was a waiting game. Norris and Bottas proved stubborn opponents, and then Ocon in the pacey Alpine with new tyres. In the meantime, Alonso was slipping down the order and the two Alpine cars sandwiched the Ferrari for a short time. An air leak on the engine of Alonso's car had contributed to his slide down the order. Leclerc eventually changed tyres and had to climb through the pack again, and another train of DRS-led cars, but with the laps now ticking by, he had to take a few more risks if he were to gain healthy points from a lost race. The safety car aided his cause as some stopped for tyres and this time, being more bold, he took both Alpines on consecutive laps, but he ran out of time to put any pressure on the Mercedes pair in fourth and fifth, Russell the nearest to him on the road. 'We know there is pace in the car. I'm not worried [about the gap in points], I'm just extremely motivated to finally have a clean racing weekend and show that we are here and we are strong,' he said after the race.

The best of the rest on this day were Mercedes. After a stick or twist situation last time out, they came out firing. The Hamilton car seemed livelier and after getting fourth place in qualifying he was the most confident he had been all year, and actually seemed very racy as he renewed his past rivalries with Alonso. George Russell started in eighth, due to a mistake on his part when he opted for slicks when the ground was damp. Engineering director, Andrew Shovlin, was complimentary of the pair, 'Lewis had a very solid drive to the podium. George also surprised us with his ability to pick cars off in the last stint.' Another corner turned perhaps, but then they did think that after Spain.

The Alpine team were left shrugging again as the engine issue for Alonso robbed him of what they thought was a legitimate shout of a podium finish. Progress had been made, though, with the front row on the grid, and if there was any doubt of the diminutive Spanish driver's popularity, it was loud and visible to see. The air leak had caused over a second a lap loss in time at its worst, and if this had not been the case, a rejuvenated Alonso could well have impacted the race placings higher up: 'The engine. That was the only answer. We tried to fix it, but it didn't work. Until that point, I think we were fighting for the podium.' The other points places were taken up by Alfa Romeo and one Aston Martin. Zhou Guanyu had the better of his team-mate in the most part but was one-upped by Stroll in the Aston Martin as the hometown driver used a one-stop strategy and held the Chinese driver back. Bottas, though, gained places when the Tsunoda crash occurred and gained an extra place when the ailing Alonso was falling back, with Zhou also able to get past the Alpine as the race came to its conclusion.

PIT STOP 1

Talks between teams and the FIA have created a further storm over the problem of porpoising. The majority of cars have suffered, some more than others, and there have been calls for a look at the new rules centring around the ground effect. The health of drivers was of paramount importance to the FIA and that is why they felt it was time to intervene in the matter. Teams were collecting their own data to present as evidence, but it was unknown just how much change to the rules could be made at this stage that would allow for a significant difference. This also led to a little bit of sniping from Red Bull team principal, Christian Horner, 'The issue with the Mercedes is more severe, or certainly has been prior to Canada. That surely is down to the team. That's within their control to deal with that. We haven't had an issue with bouncing.'

PIT STOP 2

Oscar Piastri's name was doing the rounds before Canada race weekend. The current F2 champion is being heavily linked with Alpine, but with Esteban Ocon under contract, and Fernando Alonso looking to extend his deal, there's no room in their garage, so it looks like Williams could be the final destination for the driver. Alpine boss Otmar Szafnauer said they would 'take our time and at the right moment within the silly season we'll have a look around and make those types of decisions'. His opposite number at Williams, Jost Capito, said that Piastri was 'on the list', and with Nicholas Latifi in poor form he had to dismiss reports that the Canadian could be ousted before the end of the season.

RACE RESULTS

1. Max Verstappen	Red Bull	1hr 36m 21.7s
2. Carlos Sainz Jnr	Ferrari	+0.9s
3. Lewis Hamilton	Mercedes	+7.0s
4. George Russell	Mercedes	+12.3s
5. Charles Leclerc	Ferrari	+15.1s
6. Esteban Ocon	Alpine	+23.8s
7. Valtteri Bottas	Alfa Romeo	+25.2s
8. Zhou Guanyu	Alfa Romeo	+26.9s
9. Fernando Alonso	Alpine	+29.9s
10. Lance Stroll	Aston Martin	+38.2s
11. Daniel Ricciardo	McLaren	+43.0s
12. Sebastian Vettel	Aston Martin	+44.2s
13. Alexander Albon	Williams	+44.8s
14. Pierre Gasly	AlphaTauri	+45.1s
15. Lando Norris	McLaren	+52.1s
16. Nicholas Latifi	Williams	+59.9s
17. Kevin Magnussen	Haas	+1m 08.1s
18. Yuki Tsunoda	AlphaTauri	47 laps - accident
19. Mick Schumacher	Haas	18 laps - hydraulics
20. Sergio Perez	Red Bull	7 laps - hydraulics
Fastest Lap - Carlos Sainz	1m 15.7s	

Drivers' Championship Standings

1. Verstappen	175pts
2. Perez	129
3. Leclerc	126
4. Russell	111
5. Sainz	102
6. Hamilton	77
7. Norris	50
8. Bottas	46
9. Ocon	39
10. Alonso	18
11. Gasly	16
12. Magnussen	15
13. Ricciardo	15
14. Vettel	13
15. Tsunoda	11
16. Zhou	5
17. Albon	3
18. Stroll	3

Constructors' Championship Standings

1. Red Bull	304pts
2. Ferrari	228
3. Mercedes	188
4. McLaren	65
5. Alpine	57
6. Alfa Romeo	51
7. AlphaTauri	27
8. Aston Martin	16
9. Haas	15
10. Williams	3

LENOVO BRITISH GRAND PRIX
Silverstone
52 laps - 3.659 miles/5.900km

For once, all the hype was lived up to as the drama that had been built up in the season so far was surpassed by a British Grand Prix that had everything that race fans wanted – a first-corner incident that had everyone praying, a maiden win, and a charge by Lewis Hamilton that everyone had been waiting for. This was Silverstone, and you always get a feeling that the season really gets underway when it hits Britain. Even the wet qualifying could not put a dampener on the proceedings. It looked like Max Verstappen would see the pole position plaudits come his way, even more so when Leclerc splashed through a puddle to spin so he couldn't manage better than third place. Then Sainz came through with a lap that he didn't feel was that special, but it was and it set him up for a spectacular race.

Carlos Sainz had been the victim of first-lap failures and last-lap heartache so far in this season, but at last he scored his first F1 victory, at the 150th time of asking. A long time to wait when you have a car so worthy of many wins. It wasn't plain sailing though; in fact, after the first corner it looked like being another one of those days. It was far from an ordinary day for the rookie Zhou Guanyu, his Alfa

Romeo literally turning his world upside down. The lights went out and Sainz dropped his reaction time slower than the car next to him, the champion and Championship leader, Max Verstappen. This was an instant advantage gained due to having the softer tyres, and then Lewis Hamilton was in his rear-view mirrors, as he punched a hole through the second row to climb into third place, with the first corner navigated. If those at the front were catching a glimpse in those mirrors, they may have seen the cloud of dust that was rising at the opening curve.

George Russell, not out of the top five in all the races finished so far, had a slow getaway, and had the Williams of Nicholas Latifi up alongside him. Pierre Gasly tried to squeeze into the narrow gap and that's when it happened. Russell moved to the left and tagged the AlphaTauri, which put the Mercedes helplessly sideways, and into Zhou's car; the Alfa Romeo flipped over and careened on down the straight, through the gravel trap and only started to slow when it hit the small road, at which point it cartwheeled over the tyre barrier wall, halfway up the catch fence, and dropped down, in front of startled fans. The Mercedes was damaged, its race over and was also beached in the gravel. Russell freed himself from the cockpit and immediately sprinted to the point of impact where Zhou's car lay, in a tangled mess. Upon arrival he saw that his fellow driver was moving, but trapped against the fence, he couldn't get out. Luckily there was no immediate threat of the car having any more catastrophic moments and with Russell directing the stewards over he was eventually able to get out and be taken straight to the on-site medical centre. It was a lucky escape, one which he only survived due to the halo design on the car. After the race had finished, on close inspection a neat deep groove was visible from the point where he flipped over to the gravel.

Alex Albon was also taken for assessment as the Williams had fallen foul of the accident when Bottas in the other Alfa Romeo braked sharply to avoid the debris, but ended up having the Williams also brake heavily, leading to Sebastian Vettel going into the back of Albon, sending him into the wall – and when he bounced off, he took parts of Yuki Tsunoda's car, and also made contact with Esteban Ocon. It was more like a demolition derby than an F1 race, and eventually everything stood still. Apart from the now high-waving red flags, the race was clearly going to be suspended, but this was also simultaneous with the drama ahead as down the long straight at the back of the circuit the Stop Oil protests that had been happening around the country and had threatened to take place on race day happened. Seven people were arrested as they encroached the trackside, with some getting on to the track as the cars approached. Going slower than normal race pace due to the incident, they managed to avoid the protest.

Just short of an hour was lost in time as the cars on track and the protestors off of it were all taken away. News was coming through that everyone was safe and, in particular, Zhou, who had given everyone that sickening feeling that motorsports fans around the world feel when such incidents occur. There was, though, a race still to be run, and Sainz again lined up on pole, a second chance to get the start right. A wrinkle in the rule book gave the Spaniard the lead position back, even though he was behind when the race was red-flagged. The officials have to take the restart positions of all cars following a red flag, from the last point at which it is possible to see a full order. Because Ocon and Tsunoda did not cross the safety car start line, it left the rule-makers with no choice but to revert back to the original grid order.

Verstappen now opted for medium tyres and was matched with the Ferrari duo in terms of choice of rubber, but again he got the drop on them at the start although Sainz wasn't to be fooled twice and put the squeeze on against the wall and got that little bit extra out of his car when it mattered. His team-mate was having his own tussle with the other Red Bull, as Perez got the better of Leclerc at the start but, fighting back past, he suffered some front wing damage; as Perez defended his position, he also got some damage. Bits were flying off the Ferrari and even though it was nothing terminal, one part did strike the Red Bull's nose. The pack was so tight now as they raced through the corners at scary speeds. Leclerc was forced off by Verstappen but no action was taken. This was lap one.

Sainz was ahead of Verstappen, and it wasn't long before Perez had to pit, the damage from the Leclerc debris had to be fixed, and with a new front wing he was now racing last. DRS was now activated and Max went full throttle at Sainz, with Leclerc nipping at their heels. On lap 10, Sainz, suffering with oversteer, left the door open and his race rival steamed past. It was now a case of hold on as we've seen this all before so far in 2022 – when the Red Bull hits the front, it stays there. But this is the British GP where anything happens, right? And just a few turns later the AlphaTauris were in their own personal scrap that boiled over and as Tsunoda spun he touched his team-mate; Gasly had damage and an endplate had come off.

Verstappen was heading straight for it and there was no way he could manoeuvre around it so just tried to pass over it. Instead, it somehow got stuck under the car, which led to an automatic loss of downforce. Sensing a puncture as the issue, he slowed up and the Ferrari pair were back ahead. The Red Bull pitted and were back down in sixth. With Leclerc now bearing down on his team-mate, and with his title challenge back on due to his rival's misfortune, it could be time to switch the cars, but it was too early to make that kind of decision. Another reason to hold on was the fact that a new protagonist had entered the frame. Lewis Hamilton was making his charge, after an early skirmish with Lando Norris where they had swapped places only for the Mercedes to be too powerful and take the place back. An anxious Leclerc was now pleading with his team. They put an order to Sainz to go faster; this would tow Leclerc and give some respite to his tyres. Sainz was called in for a switch on lap 20. Hamilton was now in second and the roar was louder. Then Leclerc was in, and Hamilton led the race and things would stay that way for four laps until he eventually succumbed to the wear on his boots. His stop was slow and with the Ferrari pair playing tag in their pursuit of him before his tyre change, Lewis came back out in third place.

Leclerc was now in front after that shuffle but there was another twist in the tale. Ocon was in trouble and was slowing up to an eventual halt. Lap 39 and the yellow flags fluttered and then the race was turned against Leclerc as his window of opportunity to change tyres closed, with the next four cars all deciding to come in for a tyre change and a last assault on the race. The issue was the two Ferrari cars were just too close on the track to pit them both – a double stack would be costly to the pair and the team as a whole. It was a calculated decision but one that would clearly compromise one race car more than the other. Then with orders to Sainz to hold up the pack and allow Leclerc the chance to drive away, he went against this as he rightly said that if Hamilton passed him, then it would all be in vain. Sainz was in it to win it and it didn't take long before he passed his team-mate, who on the older tyres was a sitting duck, but he wasn't going to go away easily. Hamilton and Perez were now his opponents as the race win had gone. Checo had done amazingly well amongst all the drama and distractions – consistent lap times and ease of passing the back of the pack.

Perez made the move on Hamilton, the new tyres on the Mercedes taking an age to fire up. Next up was Leclerc and that should have been easy too given the old rubber. Lap 45 now and the Ferrari was getting less grip and Perez sent his car up the inside, and Leclerc was stubborn and held on through the outside, the two going wheel to wheel as they fought for second place; as they did so, Hamilton charged up the inside of the two squabbling cars. With the loudest roar of the day, and the best move of perhaps the season so far, Hamilton was sent through from fourth to second. Perez kept the line and now had third, and was bearing down on Hamilton. It was simply racing in its purest form. Lewis was using every inch of the track, and in fact went off it, allowing both cars he had just taken back ahead of him.

Two more laps and with the race now in its final stages, Hamilton was able to reel Leclerc back in. The two were now in their own unique bubble as they swapped places, using majestic moves that the new rules had begged for. Eventually it was the DRS that caught the Ferrari out as the Mercedes was just too quick and had more grip. Leclerc was left to stave off the challenge of Norris and Alonso, and then Verstappen further back had a dance with Mick Schumacher which he could've done without as the German was racing for his first-ever Championship points. The Haas had started in 19th place and would've thought it was just another race day, but such has been his spirit in this campaign that he battled through the occasion and was greeted with overwhelming joy at the end. It was double joy for the Haas team as Kevin Magnussen drove home for tenth after only stopping once. Alpine and McLaren had been the most consistent of the midfield and the race between Lando Norris and Fernando Alonso had been a tight one, until a pit stop late on gave the upper hand to Alonso, as Norris made his change too late.

PIT STOP 1

Former world champion Nelson Piquet made headlines for all the wrong reasons during the British GP week. Lewis Hamilton, one of the sport's leading advocates in combating racism and equality, was the victim of an insult made during an interview with Portuguese television in late 2021. Piquet has been banned from the F1 paddock and had his British Racing Drivers' Club membership taken away. There was an apology, but the damage had been done, but this was no surprise to the seven-time world champion, saying it was time 'to change archaic mindsets'.

PIT STOP 2

In a trip down memory lane, Sebastian Vettel had the chance to drive the Williams-Renault FW14B car around Silverstone. Nigel Mansell had raced the car to five consecutive wins at the start of the 1992 season in which he became world champion. Vettel had made sure the car had been converted to a carbon-neutral fuel set-up and enjoyed taking it for a spin on the morning of the race. 'You can express culture in many ways, our way of expressing ourselves is driving racing cars, and it would be a shame if that was all to disappear.'

RACE RESULTS

1.	Carlos Sainz Jnr	Ferrari	2hr 17m 50.3s
2.	Sergio Perez	Red Bull	+3.7s
3.	Lewis Hamilton	Mercedes	+6.2s
4.	Charles Leclerc	Ferrari	+8.5s
5.	Fernando Alonso	Alpine	+9.5s
6.	Lando Norris	McLaren	+11.9s
7.	Max Verstappen	Red Bull	+18.7s
8.	Mick Schumacher	Haas	+18.9s
9.	Sebastian Vettel	Aston Martin	+22.3s
10.	Kevin Magnussen	Haas	+24.5s
11.	Lance Stroll	Aston Martin	+26.1s
12.	Nicholas Latifi	Williams	+32.5s
13.	Daniel Ricciardo	McLaren	+32.8s
14.	Yuki Tsunoda	AlphaTauri	+40.9s
15.	Esteban Ocon	Alpine	37 laps - fuel pump
16.	Pierre Gasly	AlphaTauri	26 laps - accident damage
17.	Valtteri Bottas	Alfa Romeo	20 laps - gearbox
18.	George Russell	Mercedes	0 laps - accident
19.	Zhou Guanyu	Alfa Romeo	0 laps - accident
20.	Alexander Albon	Williams	0 laps - accident

Fastest Lap - Lewis Hamilton 1m 30.5s

Drivers' Championship Standings

1. Verstappen	181pts
2. Perez	147
3. Leclerc	138
4. Sainz	127
5. Russell	111
6. Hamilton	93
7. Norris	58
8. Bottas	46
9. Ocon	39
10. Alonso	28
11. Gasly	16
12. Magnussen	16
13. Vettel	15
14. Ricciardo	15
15. Tsunoda	11
16. Zhou	5
17. Schumacher	4
18. Albon	3
19. Stroll	3

Constructors' Championship Standings

1. Red Bull	328pts
2. Ferrari	265
3. Mercedes	204
4. McLaren	73
5. Alpine	67
6. Alfa Romeo	51
7. AlphaTauri	27
8. Haas	20
9. Aston Martin	18
10. Williams	3

ROLEX AUSTRIAN GRAND PRIX
Red Bull Ring
71 laps - 2.688 miles/4.326km

It was loud. It was very loud. And it was very orange. The Austrian Grand Prix was always going to be a hostile backdrop for those that dare to upset the Red Bull hometown party and, in some cases, it overstepped the mark. The orange flares that go up in support of Max Verstappen always create a spectacle, a cloudy cover over the hills, and sweeping across the track. It was reported that over 300,000 fans attended the race weekend, and the majority were 'Super Max' fans and greeted their hero with raucous energy. However, there was a dark cloud looming as well. The abuse that some suffered in the grandstands was unacceptable. Ranging from homophobic slurs, sexist remarks and, in some cases, even sexual harassment, all were reported. And when Lewis Hamilton crashed out during a qualifying run, there was a cheer that is usually reserved for those winning races, not when they were still not known to be safe from a high-speed incident.

The qualifying session was fairly straightforward for Verstappen and looked like it could set a race precedent. With both Mercedes crashing out, it became a four-car race, and then three as Perez had his time wiped out for exceeding track limits in Q2 and was demoted into the middle of the pack. The Red Bull champion driver had a slack flying lap but it was still good enough to ward off his closest challengers.

This was also a sprint race weekend; given its high-speed nature and long areas of overtaking opportunity, it seemed the perfect choice. It was a chance for Leclerc to redeem himself after burning his tyres out too quick in the Imola sprint. There was Alonso not firing up and Zhou cutting out on the formation lap, meaning we had drama even before the lights went out. Verstappen on pole didn't get away cleanly and had to make Leclerc sit tight on the wall as he boxed him in, then with Sainz coming up the other side he eased back over which forced the Spaniard wider than he would've wanted, and with Leclerc now free from the vice he pushed forward, but neither red car could find a way past the RB18. With the two Ferraris now busy fighting each other for the right to combat the leader, this in turn gave Verstappen a chance to move away. But just as Leclerc had before, Verstappen was now feeling the effects of going off too quickly, his tyres feeling the pressure, so now it was a reverse situation of Imola. He had learnt after all. 'I was probably the one managing the most at the beginning and the one pushing the most at the end,' he said after the short race. Both he and Sainz could not catch the champion though, and the full maximum bonus points went to the man leading the Championship. Further down, George Russell gained a creditable fourth, and the second Red Bull of Perez used his car's superiority to climb from a lowly 13th to fifth.

This all added to the tension as the cars lined up for a pivotal race in the season. After Silverstone, no one had a chance to catch breath as they packed up and headed off to Austria. Ferrari were trying to salvage their season and Red Bull were trying to get back on the top step after missing out in Britain. If the sprint race were to go by, Ferrari had a shot, if they could keep their nerve, and their cars on the track. One thing was for sure, if the Championship was to be wrestled away from the Red Bull camp, a race win was needed here for the Monegasque . He needed to find a mean streak. Verstappen was away and clean this time as opposed to his draggy start in the sprint. Leclerc was in pursuit, and then Russell, who got a jump on Sainz, but Ferrari stayed aggressive and soon swapped the position back. Then Perez was too eager as he tried to get ahead of the Mercedes, fearing he could get bogged down and lose precious time in trying to protect his team-mate from a potential onslaught. The right rear of the Red Bull made contact with the front end of the W13 and that was enough to send Perez into the gravel but it was Russell who was also the victim, as he was charged with a five-second penalty. It looked harsh upon review but with Checo floundering and making his way back to the pits, it seemed like an even result. Eventually, though, Red Bull would retire the car – it had picked up some floor damage which just couldn't be rectified.

Back up ahead and Verstappen was having to fend off Leclerc more than he'd hoped. The Ferrari was bobbing and weaving, not going into full attack mode but doing enough to keep Verstappen busy checking his mirrors, wondering when the big move would come. DRS was helping Leclerc with each and every open flap movement but he was also making slight errors which allowed the Red Bull to keep ahead. There were too many lock-ups from the attacker, but his expertise in the braking zones was to prove too much and the inevitable happened on lap 12, as he positioned his car on the inside and rode through the corner, making Verstappen concede. Finally free of the shackles, Leclerc got away and it was Verstappen who dipped into the pit lane shortly after and opted for hard slicks. It seemed against the norm but he had to try something different as it was clear Ferrari had the edge power-wise. It wasn't long before Verstappen had passed the two cars in front, one being his nemesis of a year before – Hamilton – which was met with a huge roar. Ferrari chose to keep their cars out on track, and in doing so managed to double the amount of their lap time use on medium tyres compared to their rival. Fresh new boots on, the pair set off again in their hunt of the once-more race leader Verstappen. It was only a handful of laps later that Leclerc got past and into the front for the second time. It was odd to see Verstappen not entirely competing – he was making attempts to fend off the attacks and overtakes – but it was as if he was resigned to the fact that his race was done for the lead and he would only get the win if something happened to the Ferrari cars.

The tyre degradation on the Red Bull was excessive in contrast to other teams, something they couldn't quite put their finger on, and so a few laps after falling behind he opted for another set. And it was rinse and repeat as Ferrari stayed out much longer, able to sustain the gap enough until they both dived in on consecutive laps, and were faced with the prospect of catching and passing the Red Bull for a third time. A third time. Verstappen would never have dreamt of that. The gap with just over 20 laps to go was around three seconds. But within minutes the lead changed hands again. Leclerc was simply on a tear, and nothing was going to stop him. Sainz was tagging behind all this time and maximum team points looked odds-on, and as he was about to make his move on Verstappen there was a trail of smoke coming from the top of his car. The engine again. 'No, no, no, no …' he pleaded and agonised down his radio. It was on fire, and it was visibly a bad one and a sense of panic set in. He attempted to park the car with the flames flicking dangerously down the side of the car. Sainz stopped the car, brakes on and jumped up to leave the cockpit; as he did, the car rolled back as it was on a hill. He pushed back down on the brake, and with the car still on fire he managed to leap free as the fire marshals arrived on scene. In what seemed an age, but was mere seconds, Sainz had seen a glorious race day evaporate like the powder emitting from the fire extinguishers used to douse the burning engine.

A virtual safety car was obvious now, and all the doubts from previous races came flooding into Leclerc's head. If one engine had failed, would his too? If so, how long would he have? Would he finish the race? Then the positives as he had a fresher engine given what had happened before, so there was unlikely to be a repeat. During the VSC, the leaders went into the pits once more to see out the race. Everything checked out fine until they started racing again and there was an issue with a throttle pedal. Everyone at Ferrari was now looking through their fingers as their hands went up over their faces. They were in control for so long and now it was a case of hanging on. Hang on they did, though, and the smiles at the end were more of relief than pure joy. 'I have to admit I was nervous. I stopped watching the race in the last three laps,' Binotto said post-race. Amazingly, despite the early dominance, this was only Leclerc's third race win of the season, but one that had him back in contention just 38 points adrift with 11 races to go. Such was the pace of the lead cars, the next over the line were the two Mercedes, 40 seconds back. For Hamilton it was another trip to the podium, his third straight after the back issues that had hampered him, and Russell had fourth to compensate for his first-corner exit a week before. 'I was just watching their race on TV, I was getting a bit of a fan view of what was happening,' Hamilton said of his race and the spectacle that was unfolding half a lap ahead of him.

The Alpine cars showed good pace; even with Alonso starting from the back, he fought through the field to finish a respectable tenth to claim the last point. Ocon had one of the most straightforward drives of the day as he had a two-stop race and took his smart sixth on the grid a place higher to fifth at the chequered flag. Haas could argue they had the best result of the weekend with both cars finishing in good points places. Magnussen was eighth despite engine trouble that would cause him to lift off when he saw an opportunity to finish higher. Mick Schumacher had the better points day with his sixth-place finish that, after the super long wait to score any points, had now seen consecutive race day scores. Pierre Gasly was having a season that was becoming more and more frustrating. The talented Frenchman was hot property not so long ago but his value was decreasing as errors and car ills kept him at bay. This weekend was a sequence of misfortune. His first lap tangle in the sprint race with Hamilton saw him cruise to a 16th-place finish, only bettered by one place on Sunday in the main event; a five-second penalty for an incident with Vettel; and another five added due to track limits violations. 'We desperately need upgrades,' he said of the car.

PIT STOP 1

At last, the cost-cap saga was at an end. It was agreed by the F1 Commission that an increase to the $140m by 3.1% would help with pressures of inflation and other costs that were spiralling. This should mean that all teams would be able to compete in all races, for the remainder of the season. This was welcomed by the majority of teams but Alpine and Alfa Romeo showed little sympathy and suggested that the big-spending teams had got their way instead of cutting costs and being cautious in car upgrades.

PIT STOP 2

The Crown Prosecution Service issued a statement that confirmed it had 'authorised the charging of Bernard Charles Ecclestone with fraud by false representation following an HMRC investigation' and referred to 'his failure to declare to HMRC the existence of assets held overseas believed to be worth in excess of £400m'. Ecclestone had been a cornerstone for the best part of 40 years in F1 and had lost his top job when Liberty Media took over the sport. It is of course not the first time he has found himself in trouble with the law. A bribery charge in 2014 was settled with a £60m payoff with no guilt found, and earlier in the year he had been arrested after a handgun was found in his luggage at a Brazilian airport.

RACE RESULTS

	Driver	Team	Result
1.	Charles Leclerc	Ferrari	1hr 24m 24.1s
2.	Max Verstappen	Red Bull	+1.3s
3.	Lewis Hamilton	Mercedes	+41.2s
4.	George Russell	Mercedes	+58.9s
5.	Esteban Ocon	Alpine	+1m 08.4s
6.	Mick Schumacher	Haas	-1 lap + 5.3s
7.	Lando Norris	McLaren	-1 lap + 8.2s
8.	Kevin Magnussen	Haas	-1 lap + 11.6s
9.	Daniel Ricciardo	McLaren	-1 lap + 16.3s
10.	Fernando Alonso	Alpine	-1 lap 18.4s
11.	Valtteri Bottas	Alfa Romeo	-1 lap + 19.9s
12.	Alexander Albon	Williams	-1 lap + 24.5s
13.	Lance Stroll	Aston Martin	-1 lap + 29.4s
14.	Zhou Guanyu	Alfa Romeo	-1 lap + 31.1s
15.	Pierre Gasly	AlphaTauri	-1 lap + 38.4s
16.	Yuki Tsunoda	AlphaTauri	-1 lap + 40.1s
17.	Sebastian Vettel	Aston Martin	-1 lap + 41.8s
18.	Carlos Sainz Jnr	Ferrari	56 laps - engine
19.	Nicholas Latifi	Williams	48 laps - floor
20.	Sergio Perez	Red Bull	24 laps - accident damage

Fastest Lap – Max Verstappen 1m 7.2s

Sprint Race

1. Verstappen	26m 30.0s
2. Leclerc	+1.6s
3. Sainz	+5.6s
4. Russell	+13.4s
5. Perez	+18.3s
6. Ocon	+31.0s
7. Magnussen	+34.5s
8. Hamilton	+35.4s
9. Schumacher	+37.1s
10. Bottas	+37.5s
11. Norris	+38.5s
12. Ricciardo	+39.7s
13. Stroll	+48.2s
14. Zhou	+50.7s
15. Gasly	+52.1s
16. Albon	+52.4s
17. Tsunoda	+54.5s
18. Latifi	+1m 08.6s
19. Vettel	+2 laps
20. Alonso	0 laps – electrical

Drivers' Championship Standings

1. Verstappen	208pts
2. Leclerc	170
3. Perez	151
4. Sainz	133
5. Russell	128
6. Hamilton	109
7. Norris	64
8. Ocon	52
9. Bottas	46
10. Alonso	29
11. Magnussen	22
12. Ricciardo	17
13. Gasly	16
14. Vettel	15
15. Schumacher	12
16. Tsunoda	11
17. Zhou	5
18. Albon	3
19. Stroll	3

Constructors' Championship Standings

1. Red Bull	359pts
2. Ferrari	303
3. Mercedes	237
4. McLaren	81
5. Alpine	81
6. Alfa Romeo	51
7. Haas	34
8. AlphaTauri	27
9. Aston Martin	18
10. Williams	3

LENOVO FRENCH GRAND PRIX
Circuit Paul Ricard
53 laps - 3.630 miles/5.842km

No sooner had Leclerc fought his way back into Championship contention, the chance to wrestle it away from the current champion was threatening to vanish again. The crash into the tyre wall was one of his own making, which made the matter even worse, and as he let out a Herculean cry of anguish from his cockpit and down his radio after several huffs of heavy air, it was as if all the fight had left his body. The French Grand Prix wasn't so much won by Max Verstappen, as it was lost by Leclerc. Just 18 laps in, and he was forced to switch his engine off, his car wedged in the tyres, and admit defeat.

Ferrari were trying to outsmart their Red Bull rivals off the track as well as on it; their technical team had been looking at the optimum performance and stuck with a wider rear wing, and extra downforce with a new floor. This, it was hoped, would improve tyre life in what was going to be a hot race weather-wise. After the last race, Red Bull had to gain something extra in terms of pace and went for a more aerodynamic car, aiding its low-drag capabilities. Leclerc gained pole position; the Ferrari was proving to be a master on flying laps so far this year. His times in practice sessions and qualifying had been regularly at the top of the timing charts all year, and when he posted his flyer to gain pole he also had to thank his team-mate, who had sacrificed his session for a new power unit, giving him the perfect tow.

Verstappen was alongside Leclerc on the grid's front row, and had to stay vigilant of the quick-reacting Lewis Hamilton as the lights went out; the Mercedes man was buoyant after recent races, and seemed happier with the car, at least for now. The front three set into an early pattern, with Leclerc managing to get over the all-important one-second-ahead mark, but after the first three laps the DRS system was activated and Verstappen was on the cusp of being in range, and slowly cut the lead down to less than half a second. The early chicane in the lap was proving tricky in handling for the Ferrari and he struggled to remain in control, but kept his challenger at arm's length, with Verstappen not seeing an early chance to pass his lap times. Although consistent, they were a little off-pace with Leclerc, and so the gap opened again.

In fact, it was more a struggle for Max as he went off the track and had to be reminded of the track limits, which were being enforced more regularly now by the race officials. An early pit stop may help the cause and Red Bull called their man in, and changed for new hard slicks. Marcos Padros, Leclerc's race engineer who had dithered in some decisions, made a radio call and told the driver that Plan B was now the way forward. He had been contemplating this for a while but now this confirmation meant he could stay out and get as much from his opening set of tyres as possible and counter against Verstappen, and this would mean he would have to try and pass the leader late in the race. He had done so three times in Austria so confidence in that area was fine. The one-stop strategy was now on for both, but at vastly different stages of the race.

Both teams claimed to have the upper hand and to be in control of their circumstances, and at this cat-and-mouse stage were giving constant orders, asking questions about the car balance and feel. The drivers were happy and the race seemed to settle in for a good finish in the second half between the two. Then it happened. As Leclerc attacked the high-speed corner, the rear went from under him, his slide quickly turning into a 360 spin and straight into the barrier. After the race, Leclerc was as downbeat and deadpan as you could imagine, after having everything in control, 'Probably not enough because I went off and put the car in the wall.' The pressure that Verstappen had put on with the early stop may have been a contribution to Ferrari seeing their man have the race now under a safety car. Where the race was over for Leclerc, it now came alive for the chasing pack as they bunched up. Max had stopped but the cars behind him were still waiting for fresh tyres, and if they chose to now, he would be in no-man's land in terms of an attack.

The next four cars all swapped for hards but, as they did, Verstappen passed the safety car line and stayed ahead of his new threats. This meant that when the race got back underway, he was able to leap clear as the others were still trying to warm up and get used to the new tyres. There was a second safety car, a virtual one though. Zhou had stopped with engine troubles but in pulling off the track in a safe position there was no need for a full safety car. The race was won by over ten seconds from Hamilton, such was the clear pace in open spaces of the Red Bull. The Mercedes had been having a keen battle with Perez. The two had started on the second row but Hamilton had jumped ahead into the first corner. The Leclerc off and grouping of the field meant that Perez had a chance to get by if he could nail the restart, but the more savvy Hamilton stayed clear and Checo had to keep the other Silver Arrows at bay as he came up in fourth.

The other Ferrari of Sainz was almost a forgotten man in France due to his last row grid placing after his ten-place penalty which saw him use this as the best time to change his power unit. As expected, though, he had a super-clean drive, apart from his penalty-laced pit stop when he was slapped with a five-second penalty when he was released from his pit slot too early and almost collided with Albon's Williams. He had already reached the top ten when his team-mate went off. With his tail up and being the only Ferrari left, he was carrying their hopes of salvaging a now terrible weekend. He swiftly made up four places within half a dozen laps, his smart overtake of Russell being one of the race highlights. He now had Perez in his view and started to take time out of the gap, and just five laps later he was in DRS range.

Ferrari had the jitters on the pit wall and were concerned with Sainz's tyre wear but knew that calling him in would end any chance of him finishing higher than the place he now occupied. They dithered again asked the driver how he felt. Sainz was racing hard, the bit between his teeth and saw a chance to take Perez coming up. The call came to pit! It was too late, the Ferrari had gone past the pit lane entrance and also past the Red Bull. Then another radio call, asking him to come in on the next lap. He did so and when coming back out had lost his third place to an eventual fifth-place finish. 'We realised there was not sufficient tyre life to go to the end of the race. As simple as that,' Binotto said after. With the second

Ferrari now out of the way, Russell set about trying to get another podium finish. With the backup system in operation after a power failure on the main one, the VSC message to the teams was delayed and when Perez was expecting the slow-down message to end and go racing again, it didn't come. When it did, he didn't react in time and, as he slid, Russell floored it and got by with just three laps left. Verstappen looked back at the race win and big points lead in the standings with satisfaction, but also in the knowledge that he had been gifted both.

The Alpine and McLaren battle in the Constructors' Championship was a good one. Both cars matched up well, and the drivers on their day were either well on the pace, or way off of it. They split the next set of points between them, the Alpine pair just getting the edge. Alonso would get the better of Norris despite starting behind on the grid. 'It was a well-executed race,' Alonso gleefully said. 'We ended up just behind the top three teams in our normal position so far this year.' Ocon backed this up with eighth place, ahead of Ricciardo, this despite a five-second penalty after tangling with Tsunoda on the opening lap. The last point of the day went to Lance Stroll and he incurred the wrath of team-mate Vettel in doing so. The German had to ease up at the final corner to avoid a collision, after seizing upon a mistake by the Canadian on the last lap. 'He was obviously hitting the brakes again, so caught me by surprise, and then I lost momentum,' he shrugged. Stroll, though, claimed it wasn't reckless, so all is good.

Another pair that had to explain their actions were Latifi and Magnussen, in the Williams and Haas respectively. They clashed on lap 37, Latifi on the inside of the first corner, but he slipped wide as he went into the second turn – this squeezed the Haas over the kerbs, which led to a spin. Limping around to the garage, he would retire his car, whereas the Williams laboured on with a slow puncture and substantial damage at the rear. He too would have to retire. 'The incident was a shame as our pace was strong. We were racing against cars we knew were quite a bit quicker,' said Latifi. 'I definitely don't think I was at fault, it was maybe a racing incident.'

PIT STOP 1

This race marked the 300th Grand Prix of Lewis Hamilton's glittering career. Amazingly, he had won over a third of these, with 103 trips to the top step of the podium. Quite an achievement, and he was still going strong. 'I didn't really think much of it,' he said when told about the longevity. 'This morning I woke up feeling incredibly grateful thinking about all the people that have been with me along the way.'

PIT STOP 2

Max Verstappen opened up about the potential loss of traditional and historical circuits from the future F1 calendar. As the sport goes global and takes in new areas of interest, more street circuits have been visited. Jeddah, Baku, this year Miami, and next year Las Vegas, and already Singapore and Monaco are on the list. 'I don't want to see myself in 2028 or whatever driving only on street circuits close to the city just for the fan engagement or whatever because you need these kinds of iconic tracks on the calendar.' He was referring to the Belgian GP at Spa as it was often spoken about as being one of the first to be dropped: 'It's important to keep these really cool circuits on the calendar instead of just driving on street circuits, which I think F1 cars are not designed for anyway.'

RACE RESULTS

1.	Max Verstappen	Red Bull	1hr 30m 02.1s
2.	Lewis Hamilton	Mercedes	+10.5s
3.	George Russell	Mercedes	+16.4s
4.	Sergio Perez	Red Bull	+17.3s
5.	Carlos Sainz Jnr	Ferrari	+28.8s
6.	Fernando Alonso	Alpine	+42.9s
7.	Lando Norris	McLaren	+52.0s
8.	Esteban Ocon	Alpine	+56.9s
9.	Daniel Ricciardo	McLaren	+1m 00.3s
10.	Lance Stroll	Aston Martin	+1m 02.5s
11.	Sebastian Vettel	Aston Martin	+1m 04.4s
12.	Pierre Gasly	AlphaTauri	+1m 05.4s
13.	Alexander Albon	Williams	+1m 08.5s
14.	Valtteri Bottas	Alfa Romeo	+1m 16.6s
15.	Mick Schumacher	Haas	+1m 20.3s
16.	Zhou Guanyu	Alfa Romeo	-6 laps
17.	Nicholas Latifi	Williams	40 laps - accident damage
18.	Kevin Magnussen	Haas	37 laps - accident damage
19.	Charles Leclerc	Ferrari	17 laps - accident
20.	Yuki Tsunoda	AlphaTauri	17 laps - accident damage

Fastest Lap - Carlos Sainz 1m 35.7s

Drivers' Championship Standings

1.	Verstappen	233pts
2.	Leclerc	170
3.	Perez	163
4.	Sainz	144
5.	Russell	143
6.	Hamilton	127
7.	Norris	70
8.	Ocon	56
9.	Bottas	46
10.	Alonso	37
11.	Magnussen	22
12.	Ricciardo	19
13.	Gasly	16
14.	Vettel	15
15.	Schumacher	12
16.	Tsunoda	11
17.	Zhou	5
18.	Stroll	4
19.	Albon	3

Constructors' Championship Standings

1.	Red Bull	396pts
2.	Ferrari	314
3.	Mercedes	270
4.	Alpine	93
5.	McLaren	89
6.	Alfa Romeo	51
7.	Haas	34
8.	AlphaTauri	27
9.	Aston Martin	19
10.	Williams	3

ARAMCO HUNGARIAN GRAND PRIX
Hungaroring
70 laps – 2.722 miles/4.381km

This could be the final nail in the Ferrari season. And they only really have themselves to blame. The Hungarian GP was the final one before the summer break, a chance to end this not mathematical halfway point in the season, with a race that would set up the second half that could still bear fruit to their early season labour. Instead, they had a suspect strategy that meant those outside of their garage gained extra points, while those inside of it were getting more anxious. What it did, though, at the race end was have Max Verstappen on the podium clutching another race-win trophy, his eighth of the season, and now a lead that would be very hard to wrestle away. The fact he was anywhere near the podium at all was something of a minor racing miracle.

George Russell had gained his first-ever pole position, a little against the odds, but Mercedes will take anything that has them on top in this miserable year, by their exceptionally high standards. It was just reward for his consistent running all year; the top five placings he was securing had been a feature of this season, as much as Verstappen wins, and Ferrari drivers crying 'Noooo' into their radio. It would be hard for him to back this up on Sunday, as the car still seemed off race pace. He had the two Ferrari cars behind him, and with the champion suffering from a loss of power and no better than tenth, it looked like it could be a good day for the Prancing Horse. There was a chance of rain being detected on the radar, but cars were still on slicks, the polesitter on soft grippy tyres, whereas the red cars were both on medium sets. Sainz threatened briefly at the start of the race, as Russell left a gap, but the Mercedes was able to push on and stay ahead. With the lead intact he was able to build up a lead of close to three seconds, and then his soft tyres started to moan. The Ferrari pair were closing very fast – as expected, their car was quick. It had been all year. The pair were in tandem for the start of the race, which would make tyre stops and strategy intriguing. Sainz, though, as he was the lead of the two, was first to be called in.

He did not come in, however. Instead, the race leader did, Russell slowing down in the pit lane with a set of medium boots ready to slip on, and as he exited he had to be alert to the oncoming Alpine of Alonso. He swept around him, though, and was up to race speed in sixth position. Verstappen also came in at this point, and also had medium tyres as a preferred choice. The next lap Sainz did come in, and Leclerc now led, but the stop was slow, edging up to four seconds, and now as he entered the race again he too had to try and get past Alonso. Hamilton, who had got the jump on the Alpine cars on the grid from his seventh slot, was now up into second place, but over ten seconds behind Leclerc. We were now in the thick of all the first pit stops and Hamilton was the next major name to arrive in the pit lane, which gave his track position to his team-mate, and now he was the one chasing Leclerc, who was yet to come in. His medium tyres were now starting to show signs of wear, but a lot sooner than Ferrari had anticipated, and when he had a new set fitted just after 20 laps, he slipped out behind Russell, but ahead of Sainz and more importantly Verstappen, who was now up into fourth.

Russell's fears were now a reality as the simulations were right and they couldn't match the Ferrari pace and the lead was soon under threat with DRS activated, but Russell was canny in defence and made the second-place car fight hard. After thwarting a couple of attempts, the lead finally changed hands on lap 31, as he just couldn't cover off an attack into Turn 1. In the clean air the Ferrari could breathe, and just as we had seen on multiple occasions when it stretched its legs, it ran away. The race was becoming quite stable with the Budapest track notorious for its lack of obvious overtaking spots, and all but a handful of cars running on medium tyres. The race would become tactical in the pits, and who could get the cleanest of stops. First to blink was the fourth-placed car of Verstappen; he had gone from soft to medium, and now with a choice of any compound the team saw that the medium was reacting well and would see the race out. The stop was near-perfect, and despite now being in sixth he was feeling positive with the information he was receiving from his engineer. Russell pitted for mediums, then Leclerc pitted and had hard tyres fitted. Medium to medium to hard. It was a sequence no one else had tried to contemplate.

The first run on mediums had proved costly, and after the softs just went too quickly; the data from other cars that had run hard tyres was not favourable as they were taking their time to heat up, and left Leclerc scratching his head – at least in his mind. Now in third place, with the two ahead yet to have their second stops. With Leclerc vulnerable to a now hot Verstappen, it didn't take long for the champion to seize the moment. Turn 1 was the best chance to slide ahead, and Leclerc just couldn't respond on his still cold tyres. An uncharacteristic mistake from Verstappen meant that the race wasn't quite over, as the champion went too quick into Turn 13 and the car spun on track. There was a sharp intake of breath from all watching and those on the pit wall froze. Managing to keep the car alive, he flicked it back the right way and carried on up the track as if nothing had happened, but what did happen was that Leclerc was able to slam past.

The race within the race was back on and it only took a handful of laps before normal service had resumed as Verstappen, using the DRS down the pit straight, was able to pull the overtake at Turn 1 again. Sainz's turn to come in and another huge error as the left rear was jammed momentarily, and he was stationary for almost five seconds. Hamilton was now ahead, but as he was next in, the lead would change again. Lewis went for softs as the race was coming into its final phase, with just 20 laps to go. Ferrari were now falling apart and as Russell moved up ahead of Leclerc they had to change his hard tyres, and try and get something out of a soft set. There was a late virtual safety car – it didn't need to be a full one, which really would've spiced things up. Bottas had his race ended by a power failure, but it didn't stop Verstappen winning by nearly eight seconds. It was a race win that was completely unexpected but champions find a way to win, and this was a day when things just somehow fell into place. It wasn't a flawless win – the spin could've easily ended his race – but keeping the car going and knowing the rivals were off pace either on the circuit or off it, you take the opportunity. Behind him, Hamilton was flying on the soft tyres in the final stint. He got past Sainz, and then

Russell, the latter seeing his tyre performance starting to fade, but having enough on them to hold onto third place. From seemingly nowhere, Perez compounded the misery in the Ferrari camp by claiming fifth place.

The post-race analysis went beyond the drivers and more on the strategy, or lack of, from the teams. Praise was heaped on chief strategist Hannah Schmitz on the Red Bull wall. She had formulated the plans but was willing to adapt as things unfolded. You can have the best-made plans in the world, but if you cannot change as the race progresses, then the plans aren't worth anything. The lack of bending by Ferrari was their downfall. They could see the data but weren't willing to move from it. This, coupled with some botched stops, made for a very bad day at the office. Binotto was again fielding questions that had him shrugging and sheepishly answering, whereas Horner was smiling as he knew that his rival was choking. Over the past two months Ferrari had a competitive car, but had shot themselves in the foot with some awful calls and execution, and there had been some driver errors along the way. 'We need to get better as a whole. It always feels like there's something going on. We need to be putting a weekend together. We have to reset, analyse and to understand where we need to be better. This is extremely important,' Leclerc offered in post-race interviews.

The McLaren–Alpine fight was renewed, and this time Norris's papaya car had the edge as he got seventh place ahead of the pair but, with Ricciardo not scoring, Alpine gained more points. Norris had got fourth in qualifying and was always willing to take the race by the horns, but knew that his race wasn't at the front, and he had to let the front six go. His was largely a simple race and he just had to look after his tyres, as the two Alpine racers squabbled again. Alonso was again unhappy with his French team-mate's defence on the opening lap, which caused a scathing attack over team radio. 'Never in my life I saw a defence like Esteban today. We are in the race because of me, guys – both!' he stated. Alpine hadn't made life easy for the pair as they ran a one-stop strategy, and this meant overtime for the maligned hard Pirellis. The two clashed again following Ocon's only stop as he came out ahead of Alonso and his rock-hard slicks. It was only after team orders saved any more heated words that the former champion got ahead. 'We try to race hard always, but always giving that 1% margin to not have any accidents. We never had any and we will never have,' was the more calm response after the race, when Ocon added, 'It was just racing.' Sebastian Vettel, perhaps now racing a bit freely after his retirement announcement, grabbed the last point available on the day.

PIT STOP 1

Jamie Chadwick's consecutive race-win streak in the W Series is finally over at seven, with five races this year in the bag following on from the end of last year's two. Alice Powell won in Hungary after a very sensible race from pole to the chequered flag. Rain hit the track and forced a safety-car start but it wasn't long before Chadwick started to gain places from her low, for her, grid spot of fifth. A late safety car did give Powell a scare as it looked like the champion-elect would take top spot, but after holding her nerve and place, the last person to beat Chadwick in a race held on to beat her again. However, with a healthy 75-point lead, the title can be won in the next round at Singapore.

PIT STOP 2

Porsche is set to join the world of F1 in 2026 and details of a plan to buy in to Red Bull emerged. The move that has been ratified by Volkswagen Group, who are the parent company of Porsche, will also need to wait to see the final details of engine regulations for that season. There is a fair amount of red tape to cut through before anything formal is announced but a document revealing the tie-up suggests a ten-year deal with Red Bull with a 50% buy-in and that the partnership will also include a separate Porsche team down the line. 'There's some major caveats that we need to get past first before things can get anywhere near progression. That primarily focuses on what the final technical, sporting and financial regulations for the power unit are going to be,' Red Bull team principal Christian Horner said.

RACE RESULTS

1.	Max Verstappen	Red Bull	1hr 39m 35.9s
2.	Lewis Hamilton	Mercedes	+7.8s
3.	George Russell	Mercedes	+12.3s
4.	Carlos Sainz Jnr	Ferrari	+14.5s
5.	Sergio Perez	Red Bull	+15.6s
6.	Charles Leclerc	Ferrari	+16.0s
7.	Lando Norris	McLaren	-1m 18.3s
8.	Fernando Alonso	Alpine	-1 lap 8.2s
9.	Esteban Ocon	Alpine	-1 lap 11.0s
10.	Sebastian Vettel	Aston Martin	-1 lap 11.2s
11.	Lance Stroll	Aston Martin	-1 lap 18.8s
12.	Pierre Gasly	AlphaTauri	-1 lap 31.7s
13.	Zhou Guanyu	Alfa Romeo	-1 lap 37.2s
14.	Mick Schumacher	Haas	-1 lap 37.5s
15.	Daniel Ricciardo	McLaren	-1 lap 41.3s
16.	Kevin Magnussen	Haas	-1 lap 1m 06.2s
17.	Alexander Albon	Williams	-1 lap + 1m 06.8s
18.	Nicholas Latifi	Williams	-1 lap + 1m 18.9s
19.	Yuki Tsunoda	AlphaTauri	-2 laps + 1m 52.8s
20.	Valtteri Bottas	Alfa Romeo	65 laps - fuel

Fastest Lap – Lewis Hamilton 1m 21.3s

Drivers' Championship Standings

1. Verstappen	258pts
2. Leclerc	178
3. Perez	173
4. Russell	158
5. Sainz	156
6. Hamilton	146
7. Norris	76
8. Ocon	58
9. Bottas	46
10. Alonso	41
11. Magnussen	22
12. Ricciardo	19
13. Gasly	16
14. Vettel	16
15. Schumacher	12
16. Tsunoda	11
17. Zhou	5
18. Stroll	4
19. Albon	3

Constructors' Championship Standings

1. Red Bull	431pts
2. Ferrari	334
3. Mercedes	304
4. Alpine	99
5. McLaren	95
6. Alfa Romeo	51
7. Haas	34
8. AlphaTauri	27
9. Aston Martin	20
10. Williams	3

ROLEX BELGIAN GRAND PRIX
Spa-Francorchamps
44 laps – 4.352 miles/7.004km

If it wasn't over before this race, any hope of Max Verstappen relinquishing his Drivers' Championship was put to bed in the most emphatic way. It seems he can give other drivers a head start now. It wasn't a cocky show of arrogance, but it could have been. The tarnished-by-some title he won in 2021 was far away in his thoughts now as he took a giant step to retaining the title and stamping his authority on the sport that, if others don't catch up soon, he could dominate for as long as he sees fit.

This was a complicated weekend for the number of penalties that had even the most calculated on the grid reaching for the rule book more than once. The regularity of the penalties during the race meant you had to have a sliding scale to keep up with placings and how strategy would play a part at the end. With the race calendar showing no favourable racing opportunities in terms of overtaking, eight drivers chose to suffer grid penalties due to the taking on of new power units. Among those was Verstappen, except he went that little bit extra with a new gearbox too. His gleaming RB18 was now a different beast, the Bull in Red Bull had gotten bigger, and nastier. His grid placing was pushed forward, though, after both AlphaTauri cars were hit with issues: Gasly had electrical problems on the formation lap, so a pit lane start was required, whereas his team-mate was relegated to the pit lane after his car was seen to while in parc fermé. So now up into 13th on the grid. Just behind him was his nearest challenger in the standings, Charles Leclerc. His Ferrari had taken on a new turbo, new exhaust, new combustion engine, new electronics and a new gearbox. It was practically a new car. It was now just a case of how quick the two would make up all those lost places, and how quick the leaders could get away to make life difficult when they did get past the midfield pack.

The front was on, with Sainz inheriting pole after all the shuffling of positions, taking away a pole that was won by Verstappen, over half a second clear of new pole-sitter Sainz. It had been another session in which Ferrari had the edge, but on his opening flyer in Q3 the champion laid down a marker that no one came close to toppling. The unnerving precedent was set. And so, it was all eyes on the middle of the grid, and how well the two lead men of 2022 would cut their way through. Verstappen, as expected, got a clean start, and was ahead of the first man in front, Bottas. Latifi and Magnussen were gobbled up, before finding the stubborn Williams of Albon. Not used to the traffic that snarls up in the middle,

Verstappen and Leclerc were caught up in a mess up ahead.

The Aston Martin duo of Stroll and Vettel were scrapping, and the former went off the track and Verstappen had to work his way around, while Leclerc came off the worse of the pair. While clearing his vision and discarding a tear-off visor strip, the loose bit of Verstappen plastic had somehow found its way into the Ferrari brake duct. In a season of mishaps, what else could possibly go wrong! Of course, through the mess that the Aston Martin kicked up when it ran off line, other drivers also needed to clean their lids and so more plastic was fluttering around. It just so happened that the Red Bull one was the one, they were pretty sure, that was sucked into the Ferrari.

Then, as this was all unfolding and cars were swarming all over the track like angry wasps, Lewis Hamilton slipped behind Alonso, feeling he had a chance of an overtake on the outside, away from the racing line. Alonso held tight and hugged the kerb as he saw the Mercedes attempting an audacious move. Hamilton was level but as the turn eased into the left-hand corner, Alonso had nowhere to go. Hamilton tucked into the side of the Alpine and the tyres touched and lifted both cars full into the air and off-circuit. As they landed with a bump, Alonso was able to right his car quite quickly but swerved to avoid

Hamilton who, with the launch of his car, had gone a bit further in the air. As the Silver Arrows corrected itself and tried to race on, it was apparent that it was broken, and the car was soon parked up, with no laps completed. 'What an idiot!' breathed Alonso in his radio call. 'This guy only knows how to drive starting first!' Hamilton would later take full responsibility for the accident; after all, it had cost him more than his rival. This meant yellow flags were flying which soon went to the full safety car – not for this incident but another, as Latifi's Williams and Bottas's Alfa Romeo tagged each other and spun opposite ways. Bottas was forced into an early retirement.

It had been a breathtaking start, and with everyone still running now slowed up and behind the safety car, it was a case of gathering themselves again for the restart. However, the plastic that had got into the Ferrari car was causing problems as the brakes couldn't cool. So, a pit stop was required to clear the debris, and the standard replacement of tyres. Lap 4 and the race was back up to speed, and Verstappen in eighth place was soon past Albon and Ricciardo by the end of the lap, and then Vettel on the next one. It was non-stop and Alonso was passed with DRS assistance, and even the lone surviving Mercedes of Russell was taken with ease. It was now lap 8. Verstappen was third, and confidence was oozing through every pore. It was just the Red Bull of Perez, and the Ferrari of race leader Sainz. Would there be team orders, or would there need to be? The gap closed quickly but Perez was not going to roll over and resisted the charging number one car. Only for one lap, though, and then Sainz pitted. Verstappen was leading the race. It had happened so quickly that it was hard to assess what had happened in real time.

With the lead secured he set about opening the gap. Perez stopped for his routine change, and as he exited the pit lane he had a brief moment with Leclerc, with third place at stake, but he stayed ahead. The race leader was on the much softer tyres and the lap times showed that, but what was more remarkable was how he was able to look after them during his charge to the front. It was going against all the data that had been shown after the previous days of practice and qualifying. When Verstappen came in for his stop, the gap was sufficient that he only lost a place, to Sainz, when he left the slow-down zone of the pits, but the near five-second gap was one that would be swallowed up inside of four more laps and then when the Ferrari was prone on older tyres and with less power.

The race was won. There would be no late drama to assist any gambles that Ferrari may have for Sainz. There was now only a case of damage limitation on the scoreboard and pride to salvage. Leclerc was put onto soft tyres a couple of laps from the finish, with the single point for fastest lap in their thoughts. They misjudged the exit though, and the Ferrari came out behind Alonso and had no chance of getting by and producing the flyer, even though he did scramble past the Alpine who had recovered from the first-lap flight, to finish fifth. Or so it seemed, as the Monegasque driver was handed a five-second penalty for going over the speed limit in the pit lane. Ferrari just could not catch a break.

Perez claimed second place to complete the Red Bull 1-2. 'The pace we had with Max and Checo was enough to easily pass Carlos and bring home probably one of the most dominant performances that we've had as a team since either 2010 or 2013.' Christian Horner was keeping his emotion in check while being interviewed after the race, and everything now pointed towards a second straight drivers' title, and a break in the dominance of Mercedes in the Constructors' Championship. Of the rest, perhaps the best drive went to Alex Albon in the Williams after he claimed the last point of the day. He had already surpassed expectations when he got into the last phase of qualifying, to get ninth place and then elevated into sixth after all the shuffling. His steady race pace and good routine stops kept him largely out of trouble, and in the end, he kept his nerve when leading home a train of cars under DRS. The closest to him at the end was Lance Stroll, who rued the lost point on the early scuffles before the safety cars. 'But we had some fun battles out there within the midfield,' the Canadian smiled. Alpine jumped ahead of McLaren in their personal duel in the Constructors' Championship, but this was mainly because the British team were left hurt by a lack of straight-line speed when in the DRS zone. 'In the clean air,' Ricciardo said, 'we certainly had a bit more speed, but we just lost so much time being stuck behind cars and couldn't really make anything happen.'

PIT STOP 1

Audi are the next big name to throw their hat into the F1 ring. After years of racing at Le Mans with success, they are going to be making engines for the 2026 season. The FIA made clear the regulations for power units, which will see greater emphasis on electric power. This also paves the way for Porsche to join the party too. 'With the new rules, now is the right time for us to get involved,' Markus Duesmann, Audi board chairman, stated at a special press conference. 'After all, Formula 1 and Audi both pursue clear sustainability goals. As both our brands have a lot of fans and their special character, we decided to keep it completely separate and do two operations. We had several reasons. We will have different teams, and the powertrain has to be designed especially for the chassis. That is why we decided to split it, because we will have completely different chassis.'

PIT STOP 2

Formula 1 bosses are keen to get to South Africa, and back to the Kyalami circuits, but there will be a delay for at least one year. This means a reprieve for the Belgian Grand Prix at Spa. One of the most popular circuits with drivers and fans was said to be losing its place on the calendar. The team behind the Spa circuit have already made improvements to the track and areas around it, and will look to pump another £80m into more renovations, including the infrastructure that has a notoriously bad reputation for heavy traffic.

RACE RESULTS

1.	Max Verstappen	Red Bull	1hr 25m 52.8s
2.	Sergio Perez	Red Bull	+17.8s
3.	Carlos Sainz Jnr	Ferrari	+26.8s
4.	George Russell	Mercedes	+29.1s
5.	Fernando Alonso	Alpine	+1m 13.2s
6.	Charles Leclerc	Ferrari	+1m 14.9s
7.	Esteban Ocon	Alpine	+1m 15.6s
8.	Sebastian Vettel	Aston Martin	+1m 18.1s
9.	Pierre Gasly	AlphaTauri	+1m 32.1s
10.	Alexander Albon	Williams	+1m 41.9s
11.	Lance Stroll	Aston Martin	+1m 43.0s
12.	Lando Norris	McLaren	+1m 44.7s
13.	Yuki Tsunoda	AlphaTauri	+1m 45.2s
14.	Zhou Guanyu	Alfa Romeo	+1m 46.2s
15.	Daniel Ricciardo	McLaren	+1m 47.1s
16.	Kevin Magnussen	Haas	-1 lap + 0.4s
17.	Mick Schumacher	Haas	-1 lap + 3.2s
18.	Nicholas Latifi	Williams	-1 lap + 10.8s
19.	Valtteri Bottas	Alfa Romeo	1 lap – accident
20.	Lewis Hamilton	Mercedes	0 laps – accident damage

Fastest Lap – Verstappen 1m 49.3s

Drivers' Championship Standings

1. Verstappen	284pts
2. Perez	191
3. Leclerc	186
4. Sainz	171
5. Russell	170
6. Hamilton	146
7. Norris	76
8. Ocon	64
9. Alonso	51
10. Bottas	46
11. Magnussen	22
12. Vettel	20
13. Ricciardo	19
14. Gasly	18
15. Schumacher	12
16. Tsunoda	11
17. Zhou	5
18. Albon	4
19. Stroll	4

Constructors' Championship Standings

1. Red Bull	475pts
2. Ferrari	357
3. Mercedes	316
4. Alpine	115
5. McLaren	95
6. Alfa Romeo	51
7. Haas	34
8. AlphaTauri	29
9. Aston Martin	24
10. Williams	4

HEINEKEN DUTCH GRAND PRIX
Zandvoort
71 laps - 2.676 miles/4.307km

Mercedes was at last a credible threat, but not enough of one to stop Max Verstappen winning again. It seemed now that the only driver that could beat Max was himself, and given how much of a zone he was in, that just didn't look likely, at least not on his home patch. It was now simply a case of when he would retain his title, and not if. The gap between him and Leclerc was now over 100 points. A season that had promised so much in the first month or so had now become a showcase for his talent, as he was coming close to the single-season race-win record. Of course, a lot of this was down to the other teams just not performing to their usual lofty standards, or finding new ways to throw leads or self-combust.

He also had another pole position, which wasn't always something he could boast, but, again, through his nearest rival's eagerness to snatch the front grid spot away, he spun at a critical moment on his flying lap. It was a shame for Leclerc as he had hit top form again early in the session. So, with the two lead men in the Championship being the lead men on the grid, and with relatively equal car set-ups for the race, it could be another raid in a hometown of the best car–driver combination of the season, after Ferrari got the win in Austria. The red lights blinked out and the Ferrari got the better launch, but Verstappen had angled his car to hit the racing line into the first corner and came across to keep the lead. The Mercedes of Hamilton was trying to get in front of Sainz's red car for third spot, and did so briefly before even a glancing blow to the side of his car meant he had to check back and gather himself.

Meanwhile, Russell in the other Silver Arrows went backwards as Norris slipped past as the lap unfolded. Verstappen was fast building up a lead, as was Leclerc over Sainz who was far from staying in touch, and was falling back with Hamilton chasing, while Russell had made up the place lost on the first lap and making headway into Perez's gap. The opening furore had eased off and the front set of racers were in a settled pattern some dozen laps in. Then there was movement in the Ferrari garage, alerted by movement in the Mercedes one. It was as if they did not trust their own plans and were now very jumpy at others. No idea why, given their form …

The call did come, and it was all a bit clumsy and frantic at the same time. The call was late, which meant the crew wasn't ready and this was true to form in terms of Ferrari sloppiness. Sainz was in the pits for over ten seconds, and then to add to the scene, a stray wheel gun was bumped over by an exiting Perez. Mercedes had been pushed up the ladder into third and fourth, and were showing good race speed, with the possibility of a one-stopper on – it could be a good day, at last. This did rely on both the Red Bull and Ferrari opting for a two-stop strategy, and with two of their cars already in once, this could be on.

The other two were still out in front though, until Leclerc's softs started to wear and he too had to change; with mediums going on, it could be a risk as they would be considerably slower. Verstappen had the advantage, having been on new softs, as opposed to the used ones on Leclerc's car, but both were now on mediums, and both now sat behind the Mercedes pair. As the two raced on, it was Hamilton who scrambled for fresh tyres first, out of the race lead, then Russell followed a lap later. Verstappen was now up the road and looking good on this medium tyre, but there was no way he could make it to the end of the race on them as planned. Hamilton had also fallen behind Perez, but was on a charge.

It seemed the harder tyre was the right one, and the gamble was paying off. He had blown away the six-second gap to the Mexican in just a handful of laps, and, with it, the gap to Verstappen, which meant the timing of the leader's second stop would be crucial to the race outcome.

Halfway through the race, and Hamilton made his move on Checo, but with echoes of the year before and Abu Dhabi, the Red Bull driver knew his role here and defended against Hamilton's charge, and after ducking and edging his way behind, the Mercedes finally struck and made his move stick, but had lost time in doing so. Vettel was minding his own business as he came out of the pits, but now he was in the thick of things as the Hamilton/Perez battle was upon him. Perez went low on the banked curve, with Hamilton holding the line, forcing Vettel to yield. Perez 'the legend' had won some time back for his team-mate again; just how many times would the selfless Mexican help out with no real reward? Leclerc was up the road next for Hamilton, who was on a new tear after hitting the clean air again. The gap was down to under five seconds, so instead of taking the inevitable pass on the track, he let him go by as he sailed down the pit lane for his second stop, and after gaining the data knew that hard tyres were on to finish the race.

Red Bull were now having to face up to the fact that they had been out-thought. It hadn't happened often in 2022, so there was no real shame, but it was time to see what they could do to combat the pace. Would the hard tyre last and eventually wear, or would the pace they had sustain until the end? Lap

44 and an enforced decision had to be made. Tsunoda had just been into the pits and had hard tyres fitted. No drama there, until, that is, he reported back it felt loose. A quick check and it was fine, he was told. Confident in that message, the Japanese driver set off again, but in his readiness to retire from the car he had loosened his seat belts. The would mean a retightening, so back to the pits, but strangely they were still done up. He left the pits again, and again he called on the radio that he could feel a loose wheel causing oversteer. This time he was ordered to stop the car. This triggered a virtual safety car. This was a free stop now and Hamilton and Russell came in, as the gamble that they were on was too good to not cash out on, and slipped on mediums, whereas Verstappen, who was due to stop anyway, was now on a hard set. When racing resumed the lead was a dozen seconds, Verstappen over Hamilton, but closing.

Lap 55 of 72, and Bottas's Alfa Romeo had lost all power, with a small fire on board, and so slowly turned off the track. This time it was a full safety car. Now it was a free-for-all and anything could happen. Verstappen in, Mercedes stayed out, and out beyond the safety car line, so Max had dropped to third. The difference now was that the champion was on softs and would warm up a lot quicker and was primed for a last attack. The moment that changed the complexion of the race was when Russell made the call to come in for softs as well. The barrier between the two bitter rivals of 2021 had been removed. It was an extremely late call from the young Brit and, as the mechanics swarmed around his car, Hamilton stayed silent. Lapped cars were allowed to overtake. All lapped cars. Hamilton stayed silent. Lap 60 and the safety car was called in at the end of the lap. He would have to hold off the Red Bull for a lot longer than the one-lap shoot-out that had taken his eighth title away a few months previous. The restart had Verstappen breeze past with no extra effort needed, and with that he was off into the distance, another race win secured, and a cloud of orange smoke rising trackside. Hamilton was now being vacuumed up by the trailing pack – first his team-mate, who had left him wide open, streaked past with a hint of a touch as they blazed down the pit straight. Later, Leclerc, who had a grandstand view of the pass, suggested that they did touch, but he had no reason to stir things up, so the opinion was valid. He soon went by Hamilton too, but no contact.

Alpine continued their assault for fourth place in the Constructors' Championship. Alonso again was the star with sixth place, and this was his tenth straight scoring race. He made up for a poor qualifying, gaining seven places from his start position. It was he that was a test driver for the hard tyres as he changed early and ran well, giving out good data for all the others. His race with Norris was a good clean one, and he managed to get ahead and stay there after the last restart: 'It was 70 laps of qualifying today because we could not relax at any point.' Ocon helped the Alpine cause with a ninth-place finish. Sainz had also bumped up Alonso due to a penalty, which meant more glum faces from him at the end. His earlier pit stop disaster and an unsafe pit release (almost into Alonso) had cost him a competitive finish. The penalty gave Perez fifth place, which was scant consolation for a car that had nowhere near the same pace as his team-mate's. The last point of the race went to Stroll, as the Aston Martin felt good pace, 'I felt really confident in the car, and we were more competitive. That is really encouraging for the coming races.'

PIT STOP 1

Felipe Drugovich won the feature race over the weekend during the Dutch F2 meeting. The win means that Drugovich is 69 points clear with just two rounds left in the season and could seal the Championship at Monza. The Brazilian took the chequered flag after an eventful race that had a couple of safety cars and a red-flag stoppage. The red was shown after an incident involving F1 hopeful Logan Sargeant. Starting from third place, he had a big lock-up into the first corner and sliced through the gravel to continue racing but tagged Ralph Boschung when back on track, which put him into the barrier.

PIT STOP 2

The Dutch Grand Prix was always going to be a sea of orange. The hometown hero was setting new heights for the sport and his fans have always been loud and vociferous in their support. What happened at Zandvoort, though, was borderline dangerous, and even the man himself had some harsh words. A flare was launched from the stands and onto the track during qualifying. No one was hurt. This time. But it did cause a delay under a red flag. 'Just don't do that. It's not good for anyone, you get thrown out so you can't see the race and for us the session is stopped because it's dangerous when there is stuff on the track.' Tame words considering what could have occurred. Race promoters were more stern, saying with their statement, 'The organisation once again appeals to the common sense of all our fans and warns that the use of flares will not be tolerated.' Of course trying to police an army of 'Super Max' fans on his home patch was going to be tough, to which Sebastian Vettel simply added, 'Good luck.'

RACE RESULTS

1.	Max Verstappen	Red Bull	1hr 36m 42.7s
2.	George Russell	Mercedes	+4.0s
3.	Charles Leclerc	Ferrari	+10.9s
4.	Lewis Hamilton	Mercedes	+13.0s
5.	Sergio Perez	Red Bull	+18.1s
6.	Fernando Alonso	Alpine	+18.7s
7.	Lando Norris	McLaren	+19.3s
8.	Carlos Sainz Jnr	Ferrari	+20.9s
9.	Esteban Ocon	Alpine	+21.1s
10.	Lance Stroll	Aston Martin	+22.4
11.	Pierre Gasly	AlphaTauri	+27.0s
12.	Alexander Albon	Williams	+30.3s
13.	Mick Schumacher	Haas	+32.9s
14.	Sebastian Vettel	Aston Martin	+36.0s
15.	Kevin Magnussen	Haas	+36.8s
16.	Zhou Guanyu	Alfa Romeo	+37.3s
17.	Daniel Ricciardo	McLaren	+37.7s
18.	Nicholas Latifi	Williams	-1 lap + 42.0s
19.	Valtteri Bottas	Alfa Romeo	53 laps - engine
20.	Yuki Tsunoda	AlphaTauri	43 laps - differential

Fastest Lap – Verstappen 1m 13.6s

Drivers' Championship Standings

1. Verstappen	310pts
2. Leclerc	201
3. Perez	201
4. Russell	188
5. Sainz	175
6. Hamilton	158
7. Norris	82
8. Ocon	66
9. Alonso	59
10. Bottas	46
11. Magnussen	22
12. Vettel	20
13. Ricciardo	19
14. Gasly	18
15. Schumacher	12
16. Tsunoda	11
17. Zhou	5
18. Stroll	5
19. Albon	4

Constructors' Championship Standings

1. Red Bull	511pts
2. Ferrari	376
3. Mercedes	346
4. Alpine	125
5. McLaren	101
6. Alfa Romeo	51
7. Haas	34
8. AlphaTauri	29
9. Aston Martin	25
10. Williams	4

The New Era

THE SILLY season. A perfect description for the time of year when new contracts start being drawn up for the seats that become available each year, which are very few and far between, given that there are only 20 cars to fill and many drivers on long-term deals. Retirements, and politics, will force teams' hands when opening negotiations. And then there is the hot driver that has proven his worth in other championship series.

One of the hottest properties was Oscar Piastri. His story of getting into Formula 1 wasn't as straightforward. After winning three back-to-back championships, he was ready for the big time. His 2019 Renault Eurocup title season was backed up when he won the Formula 3 title in 2020 with Prema Racing; then in 2021, he moved up a level with the same team, and won the Formula 2 Championship, which put him in good company with Lewis Hamilton, Charles

Leclerc and George Russell as drivers that won that series in their first season. So even though this wasn't a unique situation, he was now certainly one of the new breed of talented drivers. As part of the Renault set-up in 2019, he was able to get a taste of life in F1 when he was part of the testing team for the same manufacturer, and then further testing with the rebranded Alpine team, where he was named their reserve driver.

With Alpine retaining the services of Esteban Ocon and Fernando Alonso, it looked like Piastri would have to look elsewhere to get a seat for the 2023 season. And with the struggling Williams team looking to shake up their driver line-up he was offered a way in with the British team, on a loan agreement. Then came the shock announcement of four-time world champion Sebastian Vettel retiring from the sport, which would leave a sizeable hole to fill in the Aston Martin garage.

The dominoes were now starting to fall, and Alonso was big enough to fill it and the switch was on. Now with Piastri in limbo with his employers, Alpine were keen to keep hold of their man and released a statement that quoted team principal Otmar Szafnauer saying, 'Oscar is a bright and rare talent. We are proud to have nurtured and supported him through the difficult pathway of the junior formulae. As our reserve driver he has been exposed to the team at the track, factory and testing where he has shown maturity, promise and speed to ensure his promotion to our second seat alongside Esteban.' And so it seemed cut and dried that the elevation was complete. But no one had actually heard from the young driver in this chaotic 48 hours.

That was until he took to social media and posted on his personal Twitter account: 'I understand that, without my agreement, Alpine F1 have put out a press release late this afternoon that I am driving for them next year. This is wrong and I have not signed a contract with Alpine for 2023. I will not be driving for Alpine next year.'

Not so cut and dried after all then, and now threats from the Alpine team that the matter would be solved in court and that Piastri was showing a 'lack of loyalty to Alpine' and started questioning his 'integrity as a human being'. Strong words indeed. And so there was only one way to solve this and that was for the matter to be resolved by the FIA Contract Recognition Board (CRB). Alpine were contesting that he was under contract and therefore was their driver to use in their programme, or at the very least demand compensation from other interested teams that may require his services. Alongside of this was the news that McLaren were terminating the contract of Daniel

Ricciardo; the Australian was failing to impress the team and was consistently being outperformed by team-mate Lando Norris who himself had signed a long-term deal until 2025, which meant that an attractive prospect of having two of the new guard racing for them over the next few years was on the cards if they could snap up Piastri from under the noses of Alpine.

The CRB sat in late August and established that a contract had already been agreed and signed in July by Piastri and McLaren, and therefore recognised this as the only contract that had any meaning. Upon hearing the decision, Alpine held up their hands in defeat, 'We consider the matter closed on our side and will announce our full 2023 driver line-up in due course.' Which was then followed by Piastri's own statement, 'I'm extremely excited to be making my F1 debut with such a prestigious team as McLaren and I'm very grateful for the opportunity that's been offered to me. The team has a long tradition of giving young talent a chance, and I'm looking forward to working hard alongside Lando to push the team towards the front of the grid.'

Formula 1 is always looking to push the boundaries of the sport and open doors for inclusivity in an ever-changing environment. For many years women in the sport have had to settle for a back-seat role in a male-dominated arena where for long periods of time the only way you'd see a woman trackside was handing out the champagne on the podium, or parading grid position place cards. This went well with the glamorous side that the drivers brought in the 1960s and 70s. Times change, though, and with the realisation that many good engineers were women, and they too were able to be viewed as more than a token gesture. With more women than ever before interested in the racing, it is only right that this would lead to an influx of drivers wishing to compete, and be seen as equals on the track. We are still a little way off having a full-time woman driver in the men's paddock, but that is precisely the reason a series dedicated to their skill and expertise was created.

Back in 2018, the W Series was born after being pushed around as an idea for a couple of years as a serious thought. In 2019, the first race was run with six races making up a calendar, albeit it was limited to its base in Europe with two races in Germany, as its main backer was the DTM series and the cars made up by British team Hitech GP. With 20 drivers competing, it was Jamie Chadwick who set the tone for the next three seasons, winning the first championship and then going on to retain her crown in the next two – the 2020 season was cancelled due to the Covid pandemic. However, the 2022 season was cut short due to a lack of funding and only six of the eight races were run, with the USA and Mexico dates scrapped and not rescheduled or replaced. There were some empty promises that the series would return in 2023 but instead F1 stepped in and made their own plans.

With some still criticising the W Series and its ability to be a pathway for women drivers to claim a future in F1, they set up the Academy Series which would be more akin to helping young drivers in their step up from karting and into the F3 and F2 championships. Five teams that are already established in those areas provide three cars each, making a grid of 15, with seven races that would be run on the weekends of the F1 to maintain maximum exposure. With the future of the W Series still cloudy, it was a move that was welcomed by their CEO Catherine Bond Muir, 'Our objective from the start has always been to increase the talent pool of women racing drivers, and the addition of the F1 Academy as a feeder to W Series and other series is a further step up in inspiring the next generation to progress up the motorsport ladder.'

The hard work is starting to pay off though, as triple W Series winner Jamie Chadwick announced being signed up by the Andretti Autosport team for the Indy Lights series, something that the CEO was keen to acknowledge, 'Jamie epitomises everything that W Series is about. She has seized that opportunity emphatically, securing a development role in Formula 1 with Williams, race seats in the Formula Regional European Championship and Extreme E, and now a competitive drive in the prestigious Indy Lights series in the USA. We will follow her progress closely and we wish her all the best.'

Raising the profile of women in the industry is something that Tania Brown, the club secretary of the Vintage Sports Car Club, has been championing for a long time now, 'Equality in motorsport has often felt a long way from reality especially as a young girl growing up as a marshal and volunteer. The Vintage Sports Car Club strangely was one of the few places I felt welcome on an equal footing. Being a young girl, I didn't have much exposure to other women taking part or marshalling outside my own family, my nan and my mum both having involvement on the volunteering side. At a club level, only in the VSCC did I see lots of women taking part and other girls my age had no idea that motorsport was a thing.'

With the audience now widely accepted, Tania is still a little cautious, 'Something like W Series is a slightly double-edged sword; offering something which puts women front and centre is definitely a good thing as it shows young people that it is a valid and possible choice. That said, there are certain drivers that are clearly more talented than others (although the same can be said about F1) and that leaves the series open to criticism, that people are making up the numbers. It also focuses on single-seater racing and there are many avenues open for people outside of a route to F1 which only a small handful will ever get a shot at. Progression onto the next step is also a challenge as you can be the best of the best in W Series, but with no prize drive, the next step is not obvious. All said, as exposure increases, and more women get track hours, then the quality and competition in W Series should significantly increase. If seeing women taking part in motorsport causes an increase in young girls taking up karting or other introductory formula, then we will see more women at high-level motorsport. Next step is to give exposure to other women doing well in motorsport outside of the train to F1 (GT cars for example). I can probably name more W Series drivers than F3 Championship drivers, so it is definitely increasing exposure, it is also increasing the dialogue although it is occasionally tinged with misogyny.'

SECTOR THREE

RECORD-BREAKING

Nicholas Latifi's crash led to the controversial end of the 2021 season.

Max Verstappen celebrates winning the World Drivers' Championship in Abu Dhabi in 2021.

The Michael Masi controversy led to rule changes in 2022, and ultimately cost him his job.

Fernando Alonso takes a break during early season tyre testing.

Zhou Guanyu made history as the first Chinese driver to compete in Formula 1.

The war in Ukraine caused concern and a split within the Haas team.

The Miami Grand Prix was new for 2022 and had the Dolphins NFL Stadium as its centrepiece.

The famous Las Vegas strip will provide a spectacular backdrop when it joins the calendar in 2023.

Charles Leclerc and Carlos Sainz are all smiles after they clinch a 1-2 Ferrari finish in Bahrain.

Zhou Guanyu's dramatic first corner crash at the British Grand Prix.

Charles Leclerc suffered many times during the season as his title bid stalled.

Lewis Hamilton is helped from his car after a bruising Azerbaijan Grand Prix, as porpoising issues hampered him all season.

Oscar Piastri was the centre of team rivalry during driver silly season.

Jamie Chadwick (left) was the star of the W Series, winning her third title.

Drive To Survive *brought a new audience to the sport, with executive producers James Gay-Rees and Paul Martin at the helm.*

Team principal Frederic Vasseur looks to revive Ferrari fortunes after his switch from Alfa Romeo.

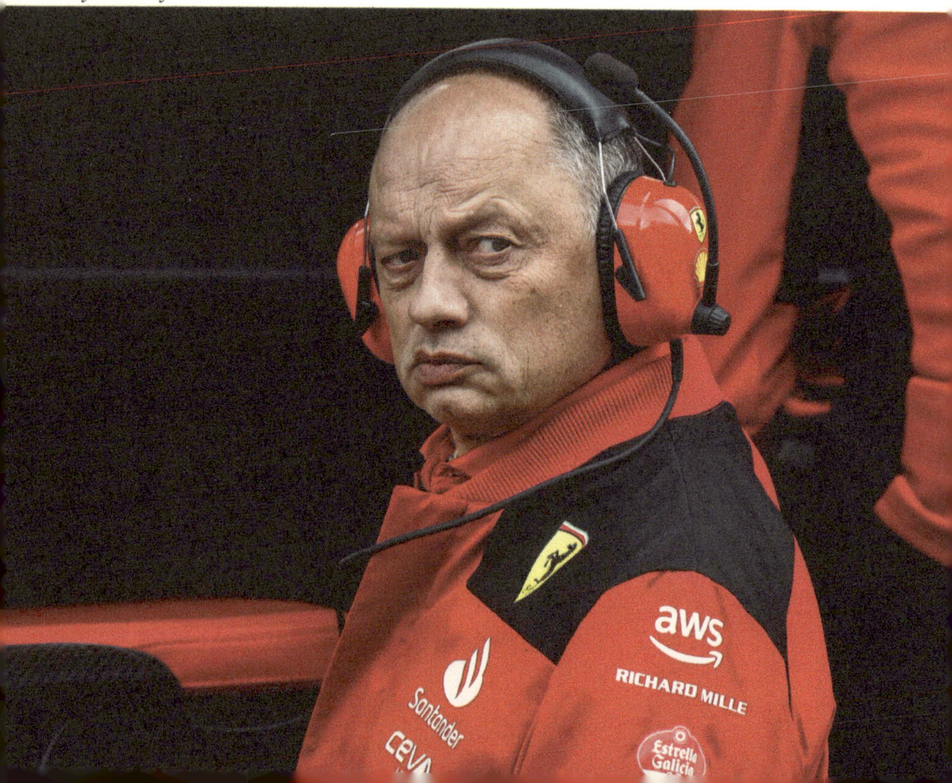

PIRELLI ITALIAN GRAND PRIX
Autodromo Nazionale Monza
53 laps – 3.600 miles/5.793km

At last Ferrari were home. This could've been a glorious homecoming if the season had ended after three races; instead they arrived on home soil in the face of much scrutiny. The Red Bull reliability that had failed them so early had been just a blip, and their season had gone on to surpass even their own expectations. They were dominant, in nearly all aspects, and had a driver that was unrelenting. Max Verstappen would take the race win; it seemed a case of rinse and repeat at each race meeting. It was down to the rest to match and then catch them.

The *tifosi* were still expectant though – some of the most passionate fans in the world were not going to give up that easily, even when the odds were stacked against them, and at this race track they certainly were stacked. Somehow, though, the RB18 was set up against the grain, with higher downforce on the car, as opposed to just letting it rip with cleaner, thinner lines. Maybe they were just adding a handicap to their machines to give the rest a sniff of a chance. Then again, they were looking at their own history and a few years ago when they had Vettel as their lead charge – he too was set up as a slow car in 2011 and won while marching to a world title. Homework done, the only blip on this replica was that Verstappen didn't hit the pole slot. This was held by Charles Leclerc, who will look back on the season and wonder how so many pole positions didn't transpire into race victories. But after a switch of engine parts, the champion was demoted down the grid to sit in the seventh space. It was a healthy, calculated move as it was the best place to make up the lost places.

Leclerc was on soft tyres to start the race got away smoothly and led into the first corner from Russell, but Norris, who started third, had a mini event when he stalled and staggered away, then Alonso and Gasly and Ricciardo were all passed by a surging Max, who had reached third place inside the first two laps. Just three more times around he was on the tail of Russell, who had no chance of defending the DRS-assisted Red Bull. And so it was a scene we had witnessed so often during the 2022 campaign. Leclerc and Verstappen, at the head of the race. The chaser was biding his time and when Vettel put his car into park mode after a dozen laps the yellow flags fluttered, and this led to a virtual safety car. Leclerc went into the pits, but only after a full lap as both he and Verstappen had gone past the pit entry before the VSC was activated. This led to Red Bull reversing their call and staying out, and when the green for go appeared, Leclerc was down in third with almost 20 seconds to find on the leader. This stop would mean Ferrari were now forced to alter their planned strategy and would have to make a second stop at some point. They were now working feverishly to find that window of opportunity.

Tyre degradation was coming into play, but not in a bad way for Verstappen. Somehow he was getting good pace, and keeping his first-stint tyres in good order, and this would only be of more detriment to Leclerc as he and the Ferrari team were trying to adjust to their new plan. With the man between the two, Russell, pitting, it was time for Max to swap his set of rubber. With a new set of medium slicks on, he set about hunting down Leclerc again, and safe in the knowledge that he would stop again, Verstappen didn't have to be in any kind of rush. Being the no-nonsense driver he is though, it just isn't in his nature to hang about and he was taking nearly a second off the Ferrari with each lap. Leclerc called time on his middle stint and had some wickedly slick softs to try and get back in the race, which even he knew would take a minor miracle to win. As always, though, there is the inevitable drama in an F1 race and so it came, as Ricciardo came to an abrupt stop on lap 46, an oil leak ending his day prematurely, and a full safety car was wheeled out.

The leaders dived in for a new set each, both softs, but the lead car was now Russell. He had to wait for the front pair to be shuffled through to the front, but there was not enough time for order to be recognised, with back markers still among the leaders waiting to get put back into place. The race would not start again and ended behind the safety car. Verstappen claimed the chequered flag, as the train of cars came around; it was his fifth straight win, and number 11 of the year. 'We are having an amazing year,' he beamed. 'And it's important we enjoy it as well.' This was not the end of a race that would appeal by any stretch of the imagination, but after the controversy of Abu Dhabi 2021, it was something teams had to be aware of under the new FIA guidelines following their investigations into that ending.

The official explanation after the race read: 'While every effort was made to recover [Ricciardo's car] quickly and resume racing, the situation developed, and marshals were unable to put the car into neutral and push it into the escape road. The race ended under the safety car following the procedures agreed between the FIA and all competitors. The timing of the safety car period within a race has no bearing on this procedure.' Yes, there was booing and jeers from the packed crowds who felt robbed of a grandstand finish, but this type of finale had to happen sometime, someplace. It just so happened that it meant that any last chance of a Ferrari scrap with their rival didn't materialise. Would the fight to the line have been a fair one if it had been restarted anyway, as Leclerc was on previously used soft tyres, and up against a brand-new set of softs on the Verstappen car? We will never know of course, but it didn't seem likely, given what we had seen for over an hour of racing, that the Red Bull car would've been passed. This also meant that Verstappen would retain his championship crown at the next race.

There was a fresh face on the grid at Monza, and he did rather well. Alex Albon was struck down with appendicitis and there was no way he could compete on race day. Nyck de Vries, who had some practice experience for Aston Martin, got a call during the practice session on Saturday, with the news that Albon was feeling rough, and could he be on standby for the Williams team, as he was a reserve for both those teams, and Mercedes. He couldn't quite make it into Q3 but had a respectable midfield start after the various grid penalties had shuffled the pack. His race speed was steady, and he settled into a one-stopper to finish ninth. Also having a good day after starting from the rear of the pack were the usual front runners of Carlos Sainz, Lewis Hamilton and Sergio Perez. The trio had all taken penalties for different power unit replacements to come home in fourth, fifth and sixth respectively. Sainz had a one-stop of near perfection, another example of how he can preserve his tyres when necessary. It would be easy to overlook, and underestimate Sainz, given his misfortune and early errors in the year, but he would bounce back so often to prove the doubters wrong. Sure, he would've liked to be winning more, but that will surely come.

We all know Hamilton's credentials and they showed again, but he had to navigate a messy first lap by the midfield and that held him up for a time. Perez equally is having to live in the long shadow of his team-mate and that means he sometimes doesn't get enough credit, but when he has to fight, we see the best of Checo. He suffered from a fire in a brake duct, caused when he collected debris very early in the race, which forced him into a two-stop plan. One team leaving unhappy was Haas, who were left feeling bruised after Magnussen was hit from behind at the first turn of the race, which led him to cut the second corner – he had no way to avoid doing so. Then, when allowing all but one of the cars back in front, as he was obliged to do, the stewards called him for a five-second penalty. Latifi wasn't let through in the Williams and it was this that he was pulled up on. Team principal Guenther Steiner raged that the team had 'got done by the officials'. Maybe it would not have changed things as they themselves messed up with an extra-long pit stop, their only one of the race, which meant that K-Mag finished last.

PIT STOP 1

It's official. The Red Bull–Porsche collaboration is off. Negotiations, after delays and uncertainty, finally came to an end. Porsche issued a statement: 'The premise was always that a partnership would be based on an equal footing, which would include not only an engine partnership but also the team. This could not be achieved. With the finalised rule changes, the racing series nevertheless remains an attractive environment for Porsche, which will continue to be monitored.' So, game over for Red Bull, but the race is not done for Porsche. 'Red Bull has demonstrated what it's capable of in F1 – as an independent team and now engine manufacturer,' said Christian Horner. Red Bull Powertrains is still an ongoing plan for 2026, and the team is open to working with Honda, should the Japanese supplier decide to make a comeback in 2026 under the new regulations.

PIT STOP 2

Felipe Drugovich finally got his hands on the F2 Drivers' Championship trophy after having to wait on the pit wall for the race to finish. After an opening-lap crash with Amaury Cordeel, he had to see if close rival Theo Pourchaire could gain any points to take it to the last race of the season. But Pourchaire finished last in the race, meaning the points gap was too large to overcome. Meanwhile, over in the USA, Will Power won the IndyCar Series title after securing third place in an exciting finish at Laguna Seca. Alex Palou got the race win from Josef Newgarden, but Power, 41, coasted home to win the title.

RACE RESULTS

	Driver	Team	Result
1.	Max Verstappen	Red Bull	1hr 20m 27.5s
2.	Charles Leclerc	Ferrari	+2.4s
3.	George Russell	Mercedes	+3.4s
4.	Carlos Sainz Jnr	Ferrari	+5.0s
5.	Lewis Hamilton	Mercedes	+5.3s
6.	Sergio Perez	Red Bull	+6.0s
7.	Lando Norris	McLaren	+6.2s
8.	Pierre Gasly	AlphaTauri	+6.3s
9.	Nyck de Vries	Williams	+7.1s
10.	Zhou Guanyu	Alfa Romeo	+7.9s
11.	Esteban Ocon	Alpine	+8.3s
12.	Mick Schumacher	Haas	+8.5s
13.	Valtteri Bottas	Alfa Romeo	-1 lap + 0.4s
14.	Yuki Tsunoda	AlphaTauri	-1 lap + 1.3s
15.	Nicholas Latifi	Williams	-1 lap + 2.7s
16.	Kevin Magnussen	Haas	-1 lap + 4.6s
17.	Daniel Ricciardo	McLaren	45 laps - oil leak
18.	Lance Stroll	Aston Martin	39 laps - engine19.
19.	Fernando Alonso	Alpine	31 laps - water pressure
20.	Sebastian Vettel	Aston Martin	10 laps - energy recovery systems (ERS)

Fastest Lap - Sergio Perez 1m 24.0s

Drivers' Championship Standings

1.	Verstappen	335pts
2.	Leclerc	219
3.	Perez	210
4.	Russell	203
5.	Sainz	187
6.	Hamilton	168
7.	Norris	88
8.	Ocon	66
9.	Alonso	59
10.	Bottas	46
11.	Gasly	22
12.	Magnussen	22
13.	Vettel	20
14.	Ricciardo	19
15.	Schumacher	12
16.	Tsunoda	11
17.	Zhou	6
18.	Stroll	5
19.	Albon	4
20.	De Vries	2

Constructors' Championship Standings

1.	Red Bull	545pts
2.	Ferrari	406
3.	Mercedes	371
4.	Alpine	125
5.	McLaren	107
6.	Alfa Romeo	52
7.	Haas	34
8.	AlphaTauri	33
9.	Aston Martin	25
10.	Williams	6

SINGAPORE AIRLINES SINGAPORE GRAND PRIX

Marina Bay Circuit

61 laps – 3.152 miles/5.073km

It had been a while, but Sergio Perez got back to the top of the podium and turned the screw on Ferrari a bit more. He was now just a couple of points off Charles Leclerc in the battle for second place in the Drivers' Championship, the title heading back into the hands of Max Verstappen who could've won it at this race weekend but was made to wait a little longer. The race had been delayed for over an hour after a deluge of rain carried through on its promise to hit.

Pole position: Charles Leclerc in 2022. He delivered again on a rain-covered track. He was pushed all the way though, in an enthralling session that had everyone guessing as to who would end up in the top slot. Leclerc had set his time, and then, when Verstappen was on his flyer, he was told he wouldn't have enough fuel to complete it and had to abort his attempt – as you can imagine, the radio airwaves turned blue quickly. The Ferrari had the other Red Bull of Perez next to him as the rain came down, and intermediate tyres were enforced upon all cars with no sign of the rain stopping. Singapore was a track where grid positioning and set-up was key, and strategy had to be nailed on. Ferrari were only ticking one of those boxes regularly in their frustrating campaign. The red lights vanished and Perez edged ahead and had the line.

With the wet weather, the braking zone decreased in size and there was no challenge from Leclerc, and so, into Turn 1, Checo seized the lead. It was a critical first move given how overtaking was going to be extremely tricky and was never easy at this circuit. Once more Ferrari were scrambling as their man had lost the initiative, but was running at equal pace with the Red Bull and the pair were easing away from third-placed Sainz. Then the first safety car, of which many had predicted a possible few, came as Latifi and Zhou scrapped over position at the back. The Canadian slid across into the path of the Alfa Romeo, pushing it into the wall, forcing an instant retirement for the Chinese rookie, and Latifi crawled back to the pits with a slow puncture. Perez led the snaking line after most had changed for another set of inters. Four laps were lost under the safety car and, when permission was given to race again, Perez was dropping way off the pace of the safety car and was more than the required car lengths behind it. When race pace was again established, it was more of the same, with no push from Leclerc, and Checo able to move away steadily, with the pair leaving the rest far behind.

Then there was a sequence we hadn't seen all season as three virtual safety cars were called in quick succession. Alonso had an abrupt engine failure, and with his car parked in an awkward position it took two laps before racing could continue. Albon caused the next one soon after as he broke his front wing having gone straight into the wall. Luckily he wasn't going too fast otherwise the damage could've been worse. With Latifi succumbing to his earlier incident, this meant both Williams cars were out. With debris on the track, the nullifying VSC allowed marshals to clean up. No sooner had they done so, another was activated. The Alpine engine on Ocon's car had enough and coughed its way out of the race with a large tail of smoke falling behind it. Thirty laps in now and everyone was hoping that a full race would still be run, and not be timed out. A new lease of life in the Ferrari saw the lead start to be cut; maybe Checo, a master of keeping his tyres in check, hadn't done so on this occasion. But then news came through of a different tyre story.

George Russell, during the VSC melee, had gone onto medium slicks. Having nothing to lose as he had started from the back of the grid with a new power unit, he was the guinea pig in a change to see if the slick tyre could make an impact, and it surely was. The track wasn't quite ready and at first it seemed a stop for inters but Mercedes were of the mind to 'try something' and a brief moment after he had to catch the car from going off. Then the dry line started to appear and, as it did, so did the quicker lap times. Like lemmings, cars started to file into the pit lane seeing the raw data that Russell was providing. Leclerc came in from second to see if he could put some pressure on the leader, but a slow stop meant the opposite. The next in a series of stop-starts to the race happened on lap 36 when Tsunoda took his car into the barriers. The full safety car again backed everyone up, and Perez was again not snug enough to the safety car. It was noted by the stewards. Lap 40 and now the medium tyres were kicking in, and the lead duo once more shook off the rest of the pack. This time, though, Leclerc was able to keep closer and the pair put on an exhibition of attack and defence. Perez was showing signs of cracking, and Leclerc was turning in one of his best races since the start of the season. Under DRS he was getting the best opportunity, but everyone knows the fight in the Mexican and how he makes his car wider when needs be, and, with the extra bit of pace in a straight line, he was keeping the Ferrari at bay. It would take a very bold move to overtake off the racing line in corners as there was still lots of surface water.

As he tried alternative ways of putting pressure on and maybe forcing an error, Leclerc was making some of his own as the laps ticked by and, on lap 48, he ran too wide and let the Red Bull escape from his DRS clutches; after that, he just couldn't find enough legs in his car to muster another challenge. The new threat for Perez at the end of the race was not from the track, but those looking after proceedings on it, in the race stewards' room. The dropping off the safety car pace, twice, was still being investigated and a possible penalty could be looming. With this in mind, the final dozen laps had Perez on the limit as he tried to create enough of a buffer should he be reprimanded, and when the chequered flag dropped he was over seven seconds ahead. The stewards after the race would slap the race winner with a five-second time penalty, but the gap was just big enough to keep him on top spot. '

'I controlled the race. The last few laps were so intense. I didn't feel it much in the car but when I got out of it, I felt it,' he commented post-race. With the 1-2 of the race pretty much locked up from the opening laps, the other race was for the last podium place, something that Sainz and Ferrari would go on to secure. It was the first time since that balmy day in Miami that two Ferraris had been in the top three. To get there, he had to see off Hamilton at the start, which was helped when the Mercedes was slow off the line. Just as Perez had gained an unassailable advantage into the first corner, the same was true for Sainz, who managed to hold off Hamilton for the first half of the race. However, that all changed when Hamilton took a bump with the barriers after a lock-up. It was a rare error, and one that would see his challenge disappear.

After a pit stop to repair the damage, he came out in fifth and a different battle. Verstappen was behind him. The focus was now on this pair as the worldwide television audience, and those around the track, had waited all season to see the two side by side on the track for an extended period of time. Given the poor qualifying session, Max had already conceded that the title wouldn't be won on this day, but knew time was on his side. He was still up for a fight, though, and had already battled through drama on the grid as he stalled and dropped to the back half of the running. Some hard but fair racing had seen him climb up to sixth place. Through the second and third VSCs he had a battle with Norris that the young Brit raised his eyebrows at, seeing his launch was almost too soon and risked a penalty. Verstappen was running hot but was also borderline dangerous. Flat-spotting his tyres with a huge lock-up that led him up the escape road and lucky not to retire, Verstappen had to pit and was now chasing on softs. Racing together and being held up a little by Vettel, the pair relived their 2021 season for half a dozen laps, and then Hamilton slipped on a wet patch and gave enough time and space for his opponent to get through. Then he managed to steal away seventh spot from another former champion, Vettel. This meant that with his points lead over Leclerc he would win the title in Japan with a win and fastest lap combo, and it wouldn't matter where his rival would be placed. Tantalisingly close.

In another dimension, the race for fourth place in the constructors' title would be as compelling as any we'd seen at the top of the standings. At Singapore the pendulum swung back in McLaren's favour as Alpine had a torrid time, and the papaya cars ended in fourth and fifth. The Renault-powered cars both exited the race before the halfway stage, and it gave a sour end to Alonso's 350th race start. Running in a comfortable sixth, he was having another measured race, but his engine let go and that was that. Ocon had similar issues and it was down to team principal Otmar Szafnauer to try explaining, 'It's important that we identify the root cause of what happened and put the measures in place to avoid a repeat. We have another race next weekend in Japan where we have the opportunity to recover.' It was also a good day for Aston Martin, as they had promised so much in this year, but rarely delivered. Lance Stroll, picking up an impressive sixth place, with team-mate Vettel in eighth, made it their best race of the season so far.

'I had a very strong start,' Vettel said. 'After that I concentrated on looking after my intermediate tyres because we knew that the track would take a long time to dry and they needed to last. I was defending for many laps, and it was a shame that Max got ahead of us on the final lap.' A down-in-the-dumps Kevin Magnussen, and his Haas team, were again looking for answers from the stewards after he was shown a black and orange flag, which means a mandatory stop for repairs. 'The team told me that the damage was minor. It was on that endplate thing, which we've explained to the FIA, it's tethered in. The FIA should know that. They make the regulations. That part doesn't come off. It's not a safety concern and here it wasn't even flapping!'

PIT STOP 1

Red Bull – the controversy never stops around them – are at the centre of a huge row involving breaching of cost-cap rules in 2021. Something they strongly deny. Max Verstappen won the drivers' title, and Red Bull finished second in the constructors' standings. They were allowed to develop their car late into the season, and now it is being questioned over its compliance to the cap rule. All teams have been told that the FIA will be looking into this as well as a discrepancy by Aston Martin. If the $145m cap has been exceeded by more than 5%, then it is considered a minor breach and could have penalties ranging from a public reprimand to points being deducted, to exclusion from events, and deductions in wind tunnel testing. An overspend of less than 5% would see similar punishment minus the public reprimand, the softer option. Red Bull have already considered the possibility of legal action as speculation from other teams piles up, 'Unless there is a clear withdrawal of those statements, we will be taking it incredibly seriously and looking at what the options available to us are,' Christian Horner said.

PIT STOP 2

There will be six sprint races in 2023, it was formally announced by the FIA, and a possibility of 30 races in total. It already has a slate of 24 lined up, with China being monitored daily due to its ongoing Covid-19 rules. There could be adjustments to the usual running order of races as well. 'The feedback from fans, teams, promoters and partners has been very positive,' F1 CEO Stefano Domenicali said of the sprint races. 'The format is adding a new dimension to Formula 1, and we all want to ensure its success in the future.' Under consideration are Bahrain, Imola, Canada, Austria, Brazil, and the Dutch races. FIA president Mohammed Ben Sulayem added, 'We concluded a thorough analysis on the impact of additional sprint sessions and have adjusted relevant parameters of our work to ensure that they continue to be regulated at the very highest level.'

RACE RESULTS

Pos.	Driver	Team	Result
1.	Sergio Perez	Red Bull	2hr 02m 20.2s
2.	Charles Leclerc	Ferrari	+2.5s
3.	Carlos Sainz Jnr	Ferrari	+10.3s
4.	Lando Norris	McLaren	+21.1s
5.	Daniel Ricciardo	McLaren	+53.2s
6.	Lance Stroll	Aston Martin	+56.3s
7.	Max Verstappen	Red Bull	+58.8s
8.	Sebastian Vettel	Aston Martin	+1m 00.0s
9.	Lewis Hamilton	Mercedes	+1m 01.5s
10.	Pierre Gasly	AlphaTauri	+1m 09.5s
11.	Valtteri Bottas	Alfa Romeo	+1m 28.8s
12.	Kevin Magnussen	Haas	+1m 32.6s
13.	Mick Schumacher	Haas	-1 lap + 1m 17.5s
14.	George Russell	Mercedes	57 laps - withdrawn
15.	Yuki Tsunoda	AlphaTauri	34 laps - accident
16.	Esteban Ocon	Alpine	26 laps - engine
17.	Alexander Albon	Williams	25 laps - accident damage
18.	Fernando Alonso	Alpine	20 laps - engine
19.	Nicholas Latifi	Williams	7 laps - accident damage
20.	Zhou Guanyu	Alfa Romeo	6 laps - accident

Fastest Lap - George Russell 1m 46.4s

Drivers' Championship Standings

1. Verstappen	341pts
2. Leclerc	237
3. Perez	235
4. Russell	203
5. Sainz	202
6. Hamilton	170
7. Norris	100
8. Ocon	66
9. Alonso	59
10. Bottas	46
11. Ricciardo	29
12. Vettel	24
13. Gasly	23
14. Magnussen	22
15. Stroll	13
16. Schumacher	12
17. Tsunoda	11
18. Zhou	6
19. Albon	4
20. De Vries	2

Constructors' Championship Standings

1. Red Bull	575pts
2. Ferrari	439
3. Mercedes	373
4. McLaren	129
5. Alpine	125
6. Alfa Romeo	52
7. Aston Martin	37
8. Haas	34
9. AlphaTauri	34
10. Williams	6

JAPANESE GRAND PRIX
Suzuka Circuit
53 laps – 3.608 miles/5.806km

It was another wet race, and one that had danger as well as drama, as some lessons from the past were not acted on properly and would lead to consternation and confusion. It was inevitable in the rain that there would be safety cars, of both the real and virtual kind. This would in turn lead to the drivers being cautious and relying on trackside assistance being more than helpful to keep them safe. Unfortunately, even though no one was hurt, there could have been a serious incident. At the end of the race, Max Verstappen had claimed back-to-back titles, even if he didn't immediately know it. With belated celebrations starting, questions and accusations were beginning to fly to find out what happened in the misty rain.

Rain. It had come down in bucketloads – not for the first time this season though, and so the show must go on. At least it would, after the debacle in 2021 at Spa, where the race was delayed and then 'won' after a few minutes behind the safety car. Teams were in agreement that decisions regarding wet races had to be made clearer in regards to points being awarded. The longer this race went on, the more it seems the set of rules fell into muddy water as no one could really pinpoint exactly the amount of points that would be awarded, but a reread of the rulebook stated that reduced points would only be handed out if the race was suspended and could not be resumed. Still a grey area, to match the colour of the sky.

When the chequered flag dropped and Verstappen had driven a superlative race to finish half a minute clear of his team-mate, the initial call on the radio from engineer Gianpiero Lambiase clouded matters as he wasn't even sure the race had finished and so Max went on. The two-hour limit had been run but the timer hit zero, which then leads to another lap to be completed. Given there was a two-hour delay to, and during, the race, the extra lap did not have to be run, and so the chequered flag hadn't been premature, even if the pit wall thought it could have been.

The order over the radio now was to complete the lap and be ultimately sure of the win. Red Bull weren't the only ones in a confused state. Then another radio message, and it was Christian Horner giving his familiar congratulations after a race win, but still no confirmation of a title. With the car parked, and exiting the cockpit, Max Verstappen greeted his crew with the usual high fives and backslapping, even pausing to visit the scales, and get a quick hug from Perez. The post-race interviews started. It was all the normal fare. Leclerc had been in a battle for second with Checo, needing Verstappen to not finish first to extend the title for one more race. Into the last lap and under pressure, with Red Bull also seeking maximum constructors' points, he cut across the chicane and kept his lead intact. This was a clear advantage though, and swiftly a decision was made to hit the Ferrari man with a five-second penalty, thus demoting him to third place. Slowly, through a loud chorus of Chinese whispers, the news of the penalty came through, and it was when the Red Bull crew started whooping again that Max broke away from his race-winning interview, to learn that it was in fact a championship-winning interview. It was the most surreal moment, and one of complete opposites to that of the previous year. Will Max Verstappen ever win a championship where there isn't a hint of drama and controversy surrounding it? That's all in the future. Now, though, the real celebrations could begin.

The wet weekend had set everyone on edge as the radar was showing showers one minute, then heavy rain the next, and would it be before the race or after it? During all the weather-watching, Verstappen had claimed pole position by the slenderest of margins from Leclerc – that in itself was a victory given the Ferrari had been a regular at the front of the grid this term. The pole didn't come easy, though, and after a spin that almost took out Lando Norris in Q3, and a lengthy wait to see if he would have his flying lap removed and suffer a grid penalty, he admitted his guilt in the mistake and was let off with a reprimand. Intermediates were enforced on all cars for a start that would not be delayed and would be a normal start instead of a rolling one. The less we saw of a safety car the better.

Verstappen was slow away and for a brief moment it looked like Leclerc would take full advantage as he got his nose in front, literally, and looked like he would lead through the first corner, but Max would not let up and kept going around the outside. He kept his nerve longer than his rival, to get back in front for a key moment in the race. As so much spray was being generated, having clear visibility was needed. It was so bad that Sainz had to back off, letting Perez through, and in trying to rectify this, he charged too hard and into a puddle which sent his car into a skid, and only came to a stop when he hit the barriers, spun back onto the track, and was fortunate not to blindside any more cars. The conditions had a price for the pack behind during the opening lap. Vettel touched Alonso and came off worse as the gravel caught him, and Zhou went on a dance provoked by no one else. Magnussen and Albon also had a brief moment and the Williams suffered a radiator leak which was terminal. That was an immediate two retirements, the Williams and Ferrari teams one car down already. Cue the safety car, and the eventual red flags, especially with Gasly limping around the circuit after gathering a large piece of advertising that was ripped from the barrier that Sainz had hit.

When Gasly got around to the pits, and exited his car, he didn't hang around to inspect any damage. The only damage he was feeling was emotional. He was clearly seen gesticulating and remonstrating with his team and anyone within earshot. Then it became apparent as to why the Frenchman was so heated. As he had to take a pit-lane start through changes to his car, he was way behind the pack when the safety car was called out, and in a bid to close he was going that bit faster than the field. However, as they all slowed to pass the recovery vehicle seeing to the Ferrari on track, he didn't see it and had to take action to avoid a collision that brought back the memory of the fatal 2014 incident that led to Jules Bianchi's untimely passing.

Gasly didn't have much time to calm down and get himself in the race zone again as the call went up that the green light would be shown again in half an hour's time. With the shower persisting, and the first-lap chaos still fresh in everyone's minds, the race was suspended indefinitely. Drivers were quite calm, some suggesting the race should go on, others just biding their time in the garage. Then an abrupt call that racing would resume and it was all hands on deck as wet tyres were mandatory and a rolling safety car restart ordered. There were enough dry areas around the track to make it work, but in the worst areas the spray would still be an issue. So, after well over two hours since the official race start time, the cars were rolling around again and it was a tentative start from Leclerc to get up to full speed that allowed Verstappen to open a gap quite quickly.

Again, though, there is always a rogue car or two that could test the water for the rest, and it was Latifi in the Williams, followed in by the Aston Martin of Vettel, that opted an immediate swap for inters. The data showed that this was indeed the better option and led to a succession of cars coming in. What followed was a processional drive from Verstappen who was gifted the bonus of a clear track in front of him equalling no spray, and a car that had got better as the season went on – or was that the Ferrari getting worse? Whichever it was, the near-half-minute gap at race end was astonishing and worthy of a championship race win. The only other item on his agenda now this year was to claim the single-season race-win record which now, at 11 race wins in this campaign, was one behind Michael Schumacher and Sebastian Vettel in that category. Not bad company to be in. Apart from the last-lap miscue, Leclerc had done all he could, given the circumstances, but he was under constant pressure which made him buckle when it mattered most just three turns from home. His fight now wasn't for the title, but for runner-up in the standings. His once-promising season had turned on its head, and now he just needed to keep his nerve, and the car on the track, otherwise the history books would show he wasn't even the nearly man in 2022, not that any prizes are given for second place. For Perez it was more than just a chance at second place, which of course would be welcome. It was also a chance to repay the faith the team had shown in him, and also to help Red Bull clinch the constructors' title and break the stranglehold that Mercedes had had on it since 2013.

With McLaren getting the upper hand on Alpine last time out, it was roles reversed in Japan as Ocon drove a fine race to get fourth, with Alonso grabbing seventh. One point would be scored by Norris, and none by Ricciardo. Starting in fifth, Ocon had to hold off a charging Hamilton late on, but did so with good skill, the straight-line speed just having enough to cover off any attack. 'I was looking more in the back than in the front in that race,' he said after. 'We knew it was going to be tough to keep the Mercs behind. I think it was a matter of time until we could really show what the car was capable of.' The double stack in the pits for the last change of the day had seen George Russell lose around ten seconds as he stood still, and this had him tumbling down the order. Only after that last stint was he able to make any real headway into the points order, and even then he lost a place on the last lap, with Alonso finding more pace in his Alpine. It was joy at last for Nicolas Latifi and Williams. He finally scored points, just two, but points. This made up for the loss of Albon on lap one for the struggling Williams team.

PIT STOP 1

Red Bull had always been confident that the FIA investigation into breaching of cost-cap rules would herald good news for the team that had become part of a war of words in the paddock and media. So when the results showed that they had indeed gone over the limit in 2021, it was now a case of how severe the punishment would be and if it would be another twist in the tale of that already incendiary season. The breach was a 'minor overspend' but could still see points deducted if the FIA wanted to take a hard-line approach. Red Bull were left 'surprised' that the outcome showed wrongdoing. The team could now sit with the FIA and discuss a deal that, if the team admit guilt to the findings, they could be hit with a lesser penalty, and they will certainly try and avoid any point-stripping that could result in Max Verstappen losing the world title.

PIT STOP 2

After the Singapore round of races, time was called on the W Series. This was down to a large American-based investor coming out of a contract. With a short deadline placed to see if the necessary funds could be raised to complete the season, it was eventually decided that Jamie Chadwick would be crowned champion in a curtailed season. Series CEO Catherine Bond Muir was optimistic that new investors would be found and was 'extremely confident' that the series would be back next year. 'We've had offers from a number of people, but the problem is getting money in doesn't happen at the shake of a money tree.' The drivers were reliant on the external funding as it meant that they didn't need to find big sponsors themselves, 'We've always said we're about finding the fastest drivers, not the richest drivers.'

RACE RESULTS

1.	Max Verstappen	Red Bull	3hr 1m 44.0s
2.	Sergio Perez	Red Bull	+27.0s
3.	Charles Leclerc	Ferrari	+31.7s
4.	Esteban Ocon	Alpine	+39.6s
5.	Lewis Hamilton	Mercedes	+40.3s
6.	Sebastian Vettel	Aston Martin	+46.3s
7.	Fernando Alonso	Alpine	+46.3s
8.	George Russell	Mercedes	+47.6s
9.	Nicholas Latifi	Williams	+1m 10.1s
10.	Lando Norris	McLaren	+1m 10.7s
11.	Daniel Ricciardo	McLaren	+1m 12.8s
12.	Lance Stroll	Aston Martin	+1m 13.9s
13.	Yuki Tsunoda	Alpha Tauri	+1m 15.5s
14.	Kevin Magnussen	Haas	+1m 26.0s
15.	Valtteri Bottas	Alfa Romeo	+1m 26.4s
16.	Zhou Guanyu	Alfa Romeo	+1m 27.0s
17.	Mick Schumacher	Haas	+1m 32.5s
18.	Pierre Gasly	AlphaTauri	+1m 48.0s
19.	Carlos Sainz Jnr	Ferrari	0 laps - accident
20.	Alexander Albon	Williams	0 laps - accident damage

Fastest Lap - Zhou Guanyu 1m 44.4s

Drivers' Championship Standings

1. Verstappen	366pts
2. Perez	253
3. Leclerc	252
4. Russell	207
5. Sainz	202
6. Hamilton	180
7. Norris	101
8. Ocon	78
9. Alonso	65
10. Bottas	46
11. Vettel	32
12. Ricciardo	29
13. Gasly	23
14. Magnussen	22
15. Stroll	13
16. Schumacher	12
17. Tsunoda	11
18. Zhou	6
19. Albon	4
20. Latifi	2
21. De Vries	2

Constructors' Championship Standings

1. Red Bull	619pts
2. Ferrari	454
3. Mercedes	387
4. Alpine	143
5. McLaren	130
6. Alfa Romeo	52
7. Aston Martin	45
8. Haas	34
9. AlphaTauri	34
10. Williams	8

ARAMCO UNITED STATES GRAND PRIX
Circuit of the Americas
56 laps - 3.400 miles/5.472km

The race win, a record-equalling 12th of the season, was greeted with mixed emotions from Max Verstappen. Yes, he was happy that he drove to another victory, overcoming a very rare mistake in the pits by his team, and that he again had the upper hand on nemesis Lewis Hamilton. It was all tinged with sadness and reflection as the Red Bull founder had passed away on the Saturday. There was no hesitation when he said he owed so much to Dietrich Mateschitz, and immediately dedicated the drive and win to him. Already crowned drivers' champion for a second time, this win and Perez's fourth place gave the Red Bull team enough points to win the constructors' title too, and stop the dominance of Mercedes and possibly start one of their own.

Pole position for Carlos Sainz added a new flavour to the start of the race – the Spaniard achieved his third pole of the year. He wasn't putting this down to late errors by Leclerc and Verstappen, although that no doubt helped. So with Ferrari at the head of the pack, it could've been a tasty afternoon in the Austin sunshine, but with his team-mate Leclerc down in the middle of the grid, and more engine components fitted resulting in another grid penalty, it would be hard work to usurp the Red Bulls. And with the Mercedes cars showing good performance and potential race pace, they were a credible potential race winner. There is a long drive up a hill at the end of the pit straight and many opportunities to pass going into the left Turn 1.

Sainz got away well but under wheelspin could not get up to pace, which left enough time and gap for Verstappen to ease past and lead the race before going down the hill. The two snaked together through the high-speed corners with the Ferrari trying to find a way back, but close behind was George Russell, too close behind, and the Mercedes front just caught the rear left of Sainz's car, causing a spin, where he had to sit and wait for the rest to slide past and then enter the pits at the end of the first lap, never to emerge again on this day. A broken radiator from the contact had meant a water leak that was beyond repair. This was so typical of everything that was 2022 Ferrari. The incident was deemed Russell's fault and the Brit was hit with a five-second penalty, which put paid to his race too.

Hamilton had gone through into second place when his team-mate was dancing with the Ferrari, but was already feeling the brutal pace of Verstappen ahead of him as the champion was away and out of DRS zone already. With one Ferrari already way back because of the power upgrade, and one further back in the garage, Hamilton was in good spirits. Another factor was that Perez was also running low in the order as he too had taken a grid penalty that had dropped him five places worse off than his qualifying speed. So, with some of his main rivals not around him, he just had the big one ahead of him. With a lead close to five seconds through the first near dozen laps, Hamilton made the first aggressive move. Medium tyres were on all cars at the start, but his first change had him slip on hard slicks. The call was maybe a bold one, but he knew that if a real challenge to win the race was on, he would have to be aggressive in decision-making as well as driving. Verstappen covered off the move by also dipping into the pit lane and adding hard tyres to his machinery. Traffic had come between the two pacesetters so patience had to be applied, as well as staying in touch pace-wise to the leader. Then other cars started to pit and this opened up the road, and when Hamilton flew up the main straight to get by Vettel, he was seven seconds off the lead and still had Leclerc to get past.

The most experienced drivers can make mistakes or be unprepared for unexpected situations, and when a gusty wind blew causing the back of Bottas's car to lose control and send his Alfa Romeo for a trip to the gravel, a safety car was called due to the unsafe position of his stricken vehicle. This led to the now often frequent sight of the cars sneaking up to each other and forming a powerful snake. Verstappen was at the head of it but his healthy lead had now gone. Leclerc took this chance to pit, a rare and welcome slice of luck that had so often been missing from the Ferrari season, and he tucked back into the snake in fourth place, behind Perez. Another spectacle that had been seen routinely over the course of the season was that of Verstappen nailing a restart, and after three slow safety car laps, he bolted away again, and was out of DRS threat, which wasn't even activated yet.

The race was to be halted again though, as Stroll and Alonso clashed. The Canadian driver was having a good race; in fact, one of his best for a long while, proving some doubters wrong. His car was strong and his times consistent. He was running behind the lead group, and down the back straight, with Alonso's Alpine behind him. The former champion was closing hard and using a great tow, he jinked left at the last possible moment, and in virtually the same moment Stroll also flicked left. In an instant, Alonso was in the air, flying, and then coming down hard on the Aston Martin's left side, causing the green car to spin wildly. Alonso bumped down to the track, and just about gathered it before fully hitting the barriers. 'We moved basically at the same time,' Alonso said after the race.

'And that was the trigger for everything. I think we saw the incident with the same eyes. Our sporting directors, they see it with completely different eyes.'

A broken front wing was the only damage, which was amazing given the visuals of the scene, and the Alpine was able to limp back into the pits. Stroll's race was done, though. There were to be plenty of repercussions from this, as Stroll was found to be at fault and handed a penalty at the next race, whereas Alonso, after his repairs, would go on to finish in seventh place. During his repairs, a wing mirror had not been spotted to be coming loose, so after several laps of racing, it came off completely and this would also be penalised but at this race, with a demotion out of the points.

So, after another safety car to sweep away the debris, Verstappen had it all to do again, and after another clean restart he wasn't getting away as easily this time. Hamilton was keeping him on a tighter leash, and DRS was looking very possible. Just as it did so, the Mercedes bobbed into the pit lane again, and the race leader covered this on the next lap. This is when the Red Bull crew for the first time in eons looked to have ended the chance of a race win. The left front was reluctant to come off, and then when it did, the replacement tyre was not going on easily. Cue the curse words, although we'd not heard them in earnest for a long time, and cue a new wheel gun. Finally, after over ten stationary seconds, he set off again. He was now off of Hamilton and had Leclerc in front of him too, which was just unacceptable given how far ahead he was when the call was made to come in. This was another slice of fortune for Leclerc who had been having an intense battle with Perez, which had meant those two had fallen way off the pace of the front two. Now, though, it had been flipped on its head.

With a third of the race left, it was now down to who had the best-performing car, as the three lead drivers all had different motivating factors for claiming the race win. Hamilton had yet to win a race this season – his W13 car was simply not good enough through the first half of the campaign, Leclerc had to salvage some pride for himself and his team, and Verstappen had to win for Dietrich. It was Max who was making the first move as he closed on Charles, and he got him with DRS assistance on the back straight, the RB18 just too powerful. And now he set about the Mercedes, cutting a lead of five seconds in half in just a handful of laps. Mercedes were confident at one stage towards the end but could see the obvious was going to happen; it was just a case of when and how as the two would not give up position easily.

Tyre strategy was now the focus and even though Max had fresher medium grip, he had spent some of this rubber while in pursuit and taking Leclerc, whereas Hamilton had relied on his second long stint on hard tyres seeing him home. In hindsight, the race was lost when Verstappen was able to get past Leclerc as soon as he did as this enabled Verstappen to close up a lot sooner than was hoped in the Mercedes garage. It was lap 50 of the 56 that Verstappen made his move – a long dive on the inside approach to Turn 12 had Hamilton defending but falling behind. It could be said his move was to avoid contact but, as he set up to stay close behind with a view to fight back, he had to concede after two more corners. The winning gap was five seconds, and Leclerc a further two seconds back holding off Perez down to the flag. 'I think Dietrich would have quite enjoyed that race from above, to see us overtaking Mercedes with six laps to go and win the constructors' title,' beamed a delighted Christian Horner.

'What could've been' was often a sentiment laid at the Ferrari garage door, and this led George Russell to apologise to Carlos Sainz after the first-lap incident that put an end to the Ferrari man's race. 'When I started attacking into Turn 1, and I saw he was on the outside of Max, I was expecting him to try to hold it around the outside. As soon as I recognised he was trying to cut back underneath Max, I had already committed to my braking zone,' he explained, 'and contact was inevitable. As a driver you need to be aware of those possibilities.' Swinging back into McLaren favour was the battle for fourth in the Constructors' Championship, this after Lando Norris drove well to claim six points. After avoiding the first lap mess, he had lost track position, and then was caught up in the Alonso–Stroll chaos. He would go past the Alpine later in the race, and the day got better for the team when Alonso was handed his broken mirror penalty. Haas were left reeling when hauled over the coals for racing with a damaged car, and felt their points position, Magnussen finishing in eighth, was justified. Two cars in the race were running with damage, but one was able to clear itself during the race thanks to a picture taken from Perez's car but Alonso did suffer. 'I fully get the argument that these parts can fly off and be dangerous,' Magnussen said, 'but if they're going to black-and-orange flag me three times, then it's very frustrating to see people have loose parts on their cars today and not get the flag.' The call for consistency in the rules was coming into question again.

PIT STOP 1

The cost-cap saga rumbles on as the initial talks between the FIA and Red Bull were postponed. This followed the death of Dietrich Mateschitz, the founder of Red Bull. Christian Horner had met with FIA president Mohammed Ben Sulayem at the start of the USA GP weekend with a view to get the talks started and get the business sorted out quickly, then the news of Mateschitz passing came through and it was agreed by all involved that the talks would be carried over for a few days after the race. This meant the deadline of any punishment was also put back. More comments had surfaced since the announcement that they and Aston Martin had overspent, with McLaren chief Zak Brown stating that the breach 'constitutes cheating'.

PIT STOP 2

The Japanese GP had many incidents, none more controversial than the on-track situation involving the tractor and crane that was removing Carlos Sainz's car after his shunt. Pierre Gasly had to slam on the brakes and swerve past the removals in a scene which could've had a very different ending. The FIA launched an immediate investigation. Several changes were made for the rest of the season to ensure this would not happen again. It was clear that the vehicle should not have been sent out on to the track when cars were still coming around to the pits behind the safety car, and that it had missed seeing Gasly still on track at high speed as he was closing the gap. There was some blame attributed to Gasly, being adjudged to have been going too fast and ignoring basic safety rules. In addition, it would end the rotation of race stewards that was put in place after the removal of Michael Masi as the only race director, with clearer messages to teams and drivers as to when any recovery vehicle would be on track, with better lighting for situations like wet-weather racing.

RACE RESULTS

1.	Max Verstappen	Red Bull	1hr 42m 11.6s
2.	Lewis Hamilton	Mercedes	+5.0s
3.	Charles Leclerc	Ferrari	+7.5s
4.	Sergio Perez	Red Bull	+8.2s
5.	George Russell	Mercedes	+44.8s
6.	Lando Norris	McLaren	+53.7s
7.	Sebastian Vettel	Aston Martin	+1m 05.3s
8.	Kevin Magnussen	Haas	+1m 05.8s
9.	Yuki Tsunoda	AlphaTauri	+1m 10.9s
10.	Esteban Ocon	Alpine	+1m 12.8s
11.	Zhou Guanyu	Alfa Romeo	+1m 16.1s
12.	Alexander Albon	Williams	+1m 20.0s
13.	Pierre Gasly	AlphaTauri	+1m 21.7s
14.	Mick Schumacher	Haas	+1m 24.4s
15.	Fernando Alonso	Alpine	+1m 25.0s
16.	Daniel Ricciardo	McLaren	+1m 30.4s
17.	Nicholas Latifi	Williams	+1m 43.5s
18.	Lance Stroll	Aston Martin	21 laps - accident
19.	Valtteri Bottas	Alfa Romeo	16 laps - spun off
20.	Carlos Sainz Jnr	Ferrari	1 lap - accident damage

Fastest Lap - George Russell 1m 38.7s

Drivers' Championship Standings

1. Verstappen	391pts
2. Leclerc	267
3. Perez	265
4. Russell	218
5. Sainz	202
6. Hamilton	198
7. Norris	109
8. Ocon	79
9. Alonso	65
10. Bottas	46
11. Vettel	38
12. Ricciardo	29
13. Magnussen	26
14. Gasly	23
15. Stroll	13
16. Tsunoda	13
17. Schumacher	12
18. Zhou	6
19. Albon	4
20. Latifi	2
21. De Vries	2

Constructors' Championship Standings

1. Red Bull	656pts
2. Ferrari	469
3. Mercedes	416
4. Alpine	144
5. McLaren	138
6. Alfa Romeo	52
7. Aston Martin	51
8. Haas	38
9. AlphaTauri	36
10. Williams	8

MEXICAN GRAND PRIX
Autodromo Hermanos Rodriguez
71 laps – 2.674 miles/4.303km

Max Verstappen had nothing left to prove this season. He had won back-to-back titles, gained victories from positions that it seemed unlikely he could win from, and had answered many critics asking if he could win and race fairly. It was a season to remember, and may not be topped for a long time by anyone, even himself. There was one more task, and that was to win one more race of the remaining three, and set the single-season win total. It wouldn't be easy as the Mercedes team had been improving steadily in the last month, and with team-mate Sergio Perez still fighting for second place in the drivers' standings, every position would be keenly contested.

One area he hadn't been dominant in this year was qualifying, but he put that right with pole position number six of the season, and was holding off a Mercedes challenge instead of a Ferrari one. After some tinkering and adjustments in Austin, the package they had was handling much better and the Silver Arrows really did look like they were flying for the first time this season in the whole session, with Hamilton in particular lighting up the timing screens. Wanting to keep his streak of a race win in every year he competed, it was a strong showing, but in pushing too hard for pole on his last run he overdid it in the opening section, couldn't recover enough and had to settle for third, behind Max and Russell, with Perez alongside him on the second row. Mexico was cheering loud for its home racer, and with their bands playing and a colourful setting, it was very much a carnival atmosphere.

Again, there was a chance of rain, something that had been way too familiar during race days in 2022, and with strategies being pored over, something that likely scared Ferrari more than the sight of a Red Bull rear wing in its front view, all weather reports were being triple-checked. In the end the rain didn't fall, which led to a simple one-stop call, and this would mean that a fairly standard race was on the cards, should there be no circumstances that would mean a safety car. No race winner for the past six outings in Mexico had won from pole position, and if anyone was to break that run it would be the champion. He had, by his admission, a poor launch, but was still good enough to keep ahead of Russell, who had tried to slip past from his opposite position on the front row. As Russell was trying to make his move, and adjust to Verstappen's to stay ahead, Hamilton had crept alongside, and erring on the side of caution, he allowed his experienced team-mate through. And Perez, who had been waiting patiently for an opening, also slipped past Russell into third place, a big cheer going up as the Brit braked too soon into the fourth corner, leaving a small window for the Mexican to squeeze through.

As often happens when drivers squabble over position in the early stages of a race, the leader can set about their own business, and already, after a single lap, the intention was set for a dominant display as Verstappen had taken out a lead that would be out of DRS range when it became available. In the opening phase, before the first pit stops, the gap would remain consistent, but with Verstappen in control of his times, before some small signs of tyre degradation. This was where not just strategy would come into play, but also tyre management, and both Max and Checo had shown in past races they could look after their sets better than most out on the grid. So, they went further than was perhaps anticipated in their first stint. This enabled Verstappen to undercut the Silver Arrows when they both stopped a few laps after. Hamilton was reluctant to change his tyres, calling to the radio that the current set was feeling good, but Perez had started to bear down on him, having made his stop, which had been hampered when one wheel nut resisted, so it was the most logical choice, given any later change would make it harder to pass as the race progressed into its latter stages. Both Mercedes were now on the hard tyre, and all the thinking in their garage was that this could lead to their first race win of the year.

As all four settled in for the long run to the end, with only just past a third race distance having been run, Verstappen was reporting to his race engineer that his gears were playing up, but of course in more colourful language. The problem was only minor, though, and likely to be just a case of the clutch not quite warming up quickly enough. So, regaining control, but not racing clear, he could watch the Hamilton–Perez battle in his wing mirrors. Every time this pair came through the grandstand area, a huge cheer went up – the Mexican was closing in as the hard tyres in the thin high-altitude air were taking their time getting hot and, having pitted earlier, Perez was benefitting with better grip. If the Red Bull could find a way through soon, he would have a distinct advantage as Hamilton would be in dirty air, and with tyres that would struggle more in keeping up. There was no attack opportunity though; the pair had had some good racing over the past year, but this time the two were stymied, even under DRS.

Under ten laps left and Fernando Alonso, who might as well have been in a Ferrari this year, for all his issues with his Alpine car, had another problem. His engine, again, let him down, and he had to retire from the race, parking up at the end of the pit straight. 'The engine cannot finish the races. I think the team have some work to do over the winter, hopefully not too much,' was all he could offer afterwards. This led to a virtual safety car, due to its location, but given that any stops now would lose track position, it was a case of stick rather than twist for the lead pack. Verstappen would win with ease; in fact, so easily that he had lapped everyone except those in the top three teams. Stunning.

Ferrari were unusually off the pace; they didn't have a great qualifying session by their standards, and on race day they didn't threaten at all. This may have been because the Mercs were muscling in, but something just wasn't right. Sainz got the better of Leclerc, but they were a minute away from the winning car, so even though they were having the better day for once, it was little consolation as the pair were way outside of the podium places. This was as, or hoped to be just a blip. 'The balance was not great. They will tell me that the car was not turning. The reason why, I think it has to be looked at and we have not a clear explanation,' a downbeat Binotto said in the post-race media glare.

The turn in fortunes was so great that Mercedes were now in touching distance of salvaging a second place from their season and once more converting

Ferrari into an afterthought in historical statistics. The battle still raged for McLaren and Alpine though, as three of their four cars scored points, and if it wasn't for Alonso's late blow-up, the blue-and-pink-liveried team could well be looking at a certain fourth in the constructors' title. It was, however, a very good day for Daniel Ricciardo. At last. This year had been a virtual write-off. He took his first-stint soft tyre to incredible distance and only stopped with a third of the race left. This had propelled him up into seventh at one stage, and then, after his stop, he managed to get back into that position to finish the race. He did have a tangle with Tsunoda which cost him, with a ten-second penalty, but this was his day and he was even helped by his team when they asked Norris to let him go so to be free to attack the Alpine duo.

PIT STOP 1

Red Bull were hit with a £6m fine and less time-testing of its aerodynamics for the next year as punishment for breaching the cost-cap budget in 2021. After denials and allegations, it was hoped that this saga would now close, and in doing so the book on the 2021 season be finally over. The wind tunnel usage would hurt more than the fine, as it is estimated that it could be 'as much as half a second of lap time' according to Christian Horner. Items that caused the overspend were noted as sick pay, staff catering, even tax benefits, all to the tune of £5.6m. Horner slammed the punishment as 'draconian', adding that 'you could burn our wind tunnel down and it still wouldn't be enough'. This was in reference to what he felt were the other teams pushing for hard sanctions on the team.

PIT STOP 2

After confirmation at the Belgian GP race weekend that Audi would be competing in 2026, they have now announced a link-up with Sauber. This tie-up was well known in the inner circle but had not been confirmed until now. 'We are delighted to have gained such an experienced and competent partner for our ambitious F1 project. We already know the Sauber Group with its state-of-the-art facility and experienced team from previous collaborations, and are convinced that together we will form a strong team,' said Audi board member Oliver Hoffmann, who is the lead of their F1 programme. Their main sponsorship deal at Alfa Romeo would end after the 2023 season, then it is expected to return to its titular name and use Ferrari power units until the 2026 season.

RACE RESULTS

	Driver	Team	Time
1.	Max Verstappen	Red Bull	1hr 38m 36.7s
2.	Lewis Hamilton	Mercedes	+15.1s
3.	Sergio Perez	Red Bull	+18.0s
4.	George Russell	Mercedes	+49.3s
5.	Carlos Sainz Jnr	Ferrari	+58.1s
6.	Charles Leclerc	Ferrari	+1m 08.7s
7.	Daniel Ricciardo	McLaren	-1 lap + 32.5s
8.	Esteban Ocon	Alpine	-1 lap + 34.7s
9.	Lando Norris	McLaren	-1 lap + 38.9s
10.	Valtteri Bottas	Alfa Romeo	-1 lap + 42.3s
11.	Pierre Gasly	AlphaTauri	-1 lap + 43.0s
12.	Alexander Albon	Williams	-1 lap + 44.9s
13.	Zhou Guanyu	Alfa Romeo	-1 lap + 56.0s
14.	Sebastian Vettel	Aston Martin	-1 lap + 59.4s
15.	Lance Stroll	Aston Martin	-1 lap + 1m 09.9s
16.	Mick Schumacher	Haas	-1 lap + 1m 18.8s
17.	Kevin Magnussen	Haas	-1 lap + 1m 20.4s
18.	Nicholas Latifi	Williams	-2 laps + 54.9s
19.	Fernando Alonso	Alpine	-8 laps - engine
20.	Yuki Tsunoda	AlphaTauri	50 laps - accident damage

Fastest Lap - George Russell 1m 20.1s

Drivers' Championship Standings

1. Verstappen	416pts
2. Perez	280
3. Leclerc	275
4. Russell	231
5. Hamilton	216
6. Sainz	212
7. Norris	111
8. Ocon	82
9. Alonso	71
10. Bottas	47
11. Vettel	36
12. Ricciardo	35
13. Magnussen	24
14. Gasly	23
15. Stroll	13
16. Schumacher	12
17. Tsunoda	12
18. Zhou	6
19. Albon	4
20. Latifi	2
21. De Vries	2

Constructors' Championship Standings

1. Red Bull	696pts
2. Ferrari	487
3. Mercedes	447
4. Alpine	153
5. McLaren	146
6. Alfa Romeo	53
7. Aston Martin	49
8. Haas	36
9. AlphaTauri	35
10. Williams	8

HEINEKEN BRAZILIAN GRAND PRIX
Autodromo Jose Carlos Pace Interlagos
71 laps - 2.667 miles/4.292km

With tears and champagne in his eyes, George Russell was on top of the podium. He had finally done it. His team had finally done it. The breakthrough moment was every bit as fulfilling as he had hoped and dreamed it would be. All the emotions came out as he stood there with the national anthem playing out, with the new words of 'God Save The King'. This wasn't the full coronation yet, but rather a confirmation that the driver who promised to bring more success to Mercedes was doing just that. His early season form suggested he was close. He didn't think it would take all year, but now it had happened it didn't matter.

The weekend started with an improbable pole position by Kevin Magnussen in the Haas. The rain came and K-Mag got his car out early enough to avoid the worst and posted a quick time that caught others on the hop. No one would go quicker before the rain got worse and ended the session in terms of no one could run quicker in the wet. It was a pole by default perhaps, but no one was more deserving of it, and the Haas team were simply a joy to watch in their garage. Under new rules, though, the pole is in the record books, but doesn't mean you start there in the main race – that position is decided in the sprint race – so

Haas knew they would not stay at the front, but just hoped they wouldn't fall too far back.

It did look like Verstappen, starting next to Magnussen, would be too much for the rest, who had aspirations of the race pole. Instead it was Russell who prevailed, as he sat nicely behind the favourite. At the halfway point of the 24-lap sprint, yellow flags were waved as Albon cruised over some debris, and after the all-clear was given, Russell took just two laps to zip past. 'We were confident we could finish second, and we thought Max would probably have quite an easy run. Max has got nothing to lose. So, he was going to be driving aggressively. It was pleasing to get the move done,' Russell said afterwards. Magnussen slipped down to eighth.

With the last upgrade, the W13 looked a different beast in Mexico, and it was enough for Lewis Hamilton to get excited about it. In a weird twist of fate, Toto Wolff wasn't present to see the weekend's events, so he didn't get to see the team's best performance of the year. This was exactly what they needed with one race to go before a winter where they would have more time to focus on what to do right, as opposed to where it went wrong. It was also a vast improvement for Ferrari, and maybe it was just a blip as Binotto had suggested last time out in Brazil. This was the race that everyone wanted throughout the year, with evenly matched teams, with drivers at the peak of their powers. The only blip this time around was the penalty that Sainz had to serve for fitting a power component; oh, and there was the mistake on Leclerc in Q3 to put him on intermediate tyres, which spoilt his session. This was standard Ferrari 2022 though. So, with Mercedes locking out the front row, they couldn't afford anything silly racing into the first corner, so there would be no fight for it. Russell got a good launch, and the pair made an early gap away from Verstappen and Perez behind them. Leclerc slipped back – choosing the medium tyre didn't seem the best decision as Norris went past – so it was a McLaren in the mirrors of the Red Bull cars. And then a safety car ruined the early action.

Ricciardo's McLaren was at fault, charging too hard to get past Magnussen in the Haas, causing the latter to spin, but then as he tried to control it, he rolled into the path of the papaya car, and put him into the barriers. It was a big shunt, at high speed, and parts of cars were everywhere. It was a huge clean-up job and took five laps to complete, the marshals doing a fine job to complete the task that quick. Usually restarts have Verstappen leading the way but it was Russell, and he got a smooth run up the straight, but equal to it was the champion and he had to lift to avoid a collision with Hamilton, who was defending position. Switching to the inside line was Perez who got a great drag, and Verstappen to the outside. The squeeze was on but the seven-time champion didn't yield and had the line – Verstappen was committed and the two couldn't avoid each other. It was the Red Bull car that came off worse – the right front wing was a mess – and Hamilton slipped down to eighth after a trip down across the run-off area. The worst-case scenario flashed through Hamilton's mind, in that he wouldn't be able to continue and that the great progress the team had made would be ruined. The car felt odd but, making quick adjustments in the cockpit, he was able to regain some balance and the car was still running. As well as having the front wing replaced, Verstappen had a five-second penalty charge for the incident. It was seen as a fairly equal blame on the drivers, but the stewards noted that Max was too fast at the moment of contact.

The next incident was more clear and obvious as Norris clattered into the side of Leclerc with too much understeer being the issue. The Ferrari hit the wall but kept it going, which stopped another lengthy safety-car routine. These skirmishes were allowing Russell to settle into a rhythm and stretch his legs a bit. His tyres were okay and withstanding the heat, and Perez was a safe distance away. His team-mate was now having to pick his way through the field and it wasn't too long before he was up to third, showing too much pace under DRS on Norris, and a Sainz pit stop gifting him the podium position at this early stage.

With pressure applied, Perez cut into the pits from second place and was out in a flash – trouble was, it still wasn't quick enough to get out ahead of the Alfa Romeo of Bottas, who held up the RB18. It was all falling into Mercedes' lap. They had many options and Russell had the key to the box. He was happy with how things were going but with the news that Perez was being impeded, he had a chance to pit and not be compromised. This put Hamilton into the lead. Just like old times. It wasn't long, however, before he too got the call for new boots, and when he came out it was behind Sainz. Both Silver Arrows were reacting well to their new medium tyres, and having inherited third again from Sainz's next stop, Hamilton was free to go after Perez. Lap 44 was when the 1-2 was back on as, with DRS, Hamilton breezed past Perez. It really was going their way when Checo had another set of boots fitted and this left the lead pair way out in front with a chance of an undercut pit stop.

Mercedes slightly misjudged with Hamilton as he came out behind Sainz, who was on much older tyres, but they got Russell out ahead, just. Then the McLaren of Norris made it an awful day for that team as a glitch in the system put an end to their afternoon, and, as he parked up, the need for a virtual safety car was made. Sainz dived in once more and got some softs bolted on, which could cause a surprise, and he was even more hopeful when the safety car made another appearance, and this of course backed everyone up with all lapped cars going past and around. Hamilton had some flashbacks as he sat in his car waiting for the race to go green again. Some cars behind were on much fresher tyres and he could be swallowed up. It was time to race again though, and not time to worry. Nailing the restart, Russell was away, and Hamilton dropped in behind him. The next few laps were all about concentration and seeing it to the line. Russell was about to be a first-time Grand Prix winner, and he started to recall all the moments that got him there. Family, sponsors, team-mates old and new, staff – his mental checklist was long but he ticked every box. Remarkably, he had won the race with a broken car: the last few laps it had no cooling system as there was a water leak. The team decided to keep this from him. This was as good a 1-2 as the team had ever had, after the long, arduous year, with the car bouncing, and drivers nursing backaches.

Leclerc, knowing how close the championship battle with Perez was, had been keen for his team-mate to swap positions. It was a call that was repeated time and again, but there was no order. The pair were free to race. Sainz would not give up his position on track unless told to do so, and he ended up in third, with Leclerc immediately behind him as they finished. Team orders were a hot and contentious issue, and with Ferrari allowing their duo to race freely, Red Bull were being more hospitable where championship points and placings were concerned. Verstappen had been on one of his typical charges without ever threatening to get onto the podium. His race was more of pride, and showmanship. Perez didn't fight him when he went past, and when it became apparent that Max would not get to the Ferrari pair, Checo asked if he would give his place back, as he needed the points in the battle with Leclerc. He was told that would happen. Verstappen was asked to allow a pass, and the reason why. He did not. Perez asked again but more in anguish, the Mexican clearly letting his feelings known, 'After all I've done for him, it's a bit disappointing. I'm really surprised.' 'I have my reasons,' Verstappen hit back. This was all playing out live as the two were on the in-lap. Could this go back as far as Monaco this year when a Perez spin in Q3 red-flagged the session as Max was on a flyer? For all the good clean racing, and turning of a page that the champion had done this year, he ripped the one out that said take one for the team. Was he showing everyone who was in charge, and where the line is drawn? Either way this was bad press for the now two-time champion, and another headache for the Red Bull team to deal with.

It seemed like a good day for Alpine, who had now all but secured fourth in the Constructors' Championship. Both McLaren cars went out of the race and Alonso had a great drive to finish fifth. For once, his engine did not blow up. It was not all fun and games, though, as the start of the sprint race was marred when the two almost touched, and then did when Ocon was too tight through Turn 4, causing Alonso to slip and slide but keep going. The two cars went at it again, this time the Spanish driving nipping away at the Frenchman. This bad feeling carried over into the main race and Alonso went bold with a three-stop call, and got his wish with a late safety car, and when in ninth on the restart wanted Ocon to get the call to let him past. With Vettel up ahead, Ocon wanted his chance to take on the Aston Martin, and then move over. He did so, but cost Alonso some time. His high-place finish could have been better, but no one will ever know. 'I just want to go to Abu Dhabi and test the green car,' Alonso said after the sprint race, referring to his impending move to Aston Martin. Bottas edged out the Aston Martin cars to bag ninth place ahead of Stroll, then Vettel. 'We could have been higher but the safety car at the end didn't really play in our favour. It left us exposed,' the Finn said.

PIT STOP 1

Ross Brawn, a well-respected man, a trusted man, has said the sprint format race weekend could have changes going into 2023. After the last of the three sprints was staged in Brazil, he addressed how it could be altered going into the new season: 'We'd be very cautious about changing things, and I don't think we should move to a dramatically different format. It was a fantastic race. It gave the crowds terrific entertainment. Qualifying's special, but not as special as that was today.' His comments came after the best of the sprints in 2022. The drivers, though, including champion Max Verstappen, had expressed concerns, 'Overall, you don't see a lot of overtaking unless a car is out of position. So, then it's not really that fun for me,' he said dryly.

PIT STOP 2

The fallout from the race orders that Red Bull gave that were not adhered to will linger in the minds of many, not least Sergio Perez. The situation was so heated that an emergency meeting was held with the two drivers, Christian Horner, and adviser Helmut Marko. 'We put everything on the table,' champion Verstappen said. The team were keen to squash what happened quickly, they didn't need extra drama after the year they'd had. It was a confusing situation that developed on the track, with Max given the order to let Checo through as he chased crucial points in his battle with Charles Leclerc for second in the Championship. 'It shows who he really is,' Perez told reporters, before the meeting. It has been resolved, at least for now. As for the next time team orders are issued, let's wait and see …

RACE RESULTS

1.	George Russell	Mercedes	1hr 38m 34.0s
2.	Lewis Hamilton	Mercedes	+1.5s
3.	Carlos Sainz Jnr	Ferrari	+4.0s
4.	Charles Leclerc	Ferrari	+8.4s
5.	Fernando Alonso	Alpine	+9.5s
6.	Max Verstappen	Red Bull	+10.0s
7.	Sergio Perez	Red Bull	+14.0s
8.	Esteban Ocon	Alpine	+18.6s
9.	Valtteri Bottas	Alfa Romeo	+22.5s
10.	Lance Stroll	Aston Martin	+23.5s
11.	Sebastian Vettel	Aston Martin	+26.1s
12.	Zhou Guanyu	Alfa Romeo	+29.3s
13.	Mick Schumacher	Haas	+29.8s
14.	Pierre Gasly	AlphaTauri	+31.8s
15.	Alexander Albon	Williams	+36.0s
16.	Nicholas Latifi	Williams	+37.0s
17.	Yuki Tsunoda	AlphaTauri	-1 lap + 32.3s
18.	Lando Norris	McLaren	50 laps - lost power
19.	Kevin Magnussen	Haas	0 laps - accident
20.	Daniel Ricciardo	McLaren	0 laps - accident

Fastest Lap - George Russell 1m 13.7s

Sprint RACE RESULTS

1. Russell	30m 11.3s
2. Sainz	+3.9s
3. Hamilton	+4.4s
4. Verstappen	+10.4s
5. Perez	+11.8s
6. Leclerc	+13.1s
7. Norris	+25.6s
8. Magnussen	+28.7s
9. Vettel	+30.2s
10. Gasly	+34.1s
11. Ricciardo	+39.3s
12. Schumacher	+41.1s
13. Zhou	+41.7s
14. Bottas	+42.3s
15. Tsunoda	+50.3s
16. Stroll	+50.7s
17. Ocon	+51.7s
18. Alonso	+53.9s
19. Latifi	+1m 16.8s
20. Albon	12 laps – hit debris

Drivers' Championship Standings

1.	Verstappen	429pts
2.	Leclerc	290
3.	Perez	290
4.	Russell	265
5.	Hamilton	240
6.	Sainz	234
7.	Norris	113
8.	Ocon	86
9.	Alonso	81
10.	Bottas	49
11.	Vettel	36
12.	Ricciardo	35
13.	Magnussen	25
14.	Gasly	23
15.	Stroll	14
16.	Schumacher	12
17.	Tsunoda	12
18.	Zhou	6
19.	Albon	4
20.	Latifi	2
21.	De Vries	2

Constructors' Championship Standings

1.	Red Bull	719pts
2.	Ferrari	524
3.	Mercedes	505
4.	Alpine	167
5.	McLaren	148
6.	Alfa Romeo	55
7.	Aston Martin	50
8.	Haas	37
9.	AlphaTauri	35
10.	Williams	8

ETIHAD AIRWAYS ABU DHABI GRAND PRIX

Yas Marina Circuit

58 laps – 3.281 miles/5.281km

And so, it was back to the scene of the most controversial ending to a Formula 1 season in its history, and the scene of another Max Verstappen win; this time, though, there were no major headlines – unless you create one that shows that Verstappen has had one of the most dominant seasons of any driver, perhaps ever. Yes, there have been the Schumacher years, and the Vettel campaigns, but 2022 was one where the champion was dominant. The car itself had its issues, and even through those early stages Max didn't throw his toys out the box completely. He stuck with it, and where others were either breaking down, or bouncing around, he won race, after race, after race.

After the bad taste left in the mouth as they left Brazil, Red Bull squared off the front row – Max at the top, and Sergio Perez next to him. The champion had even made sure of this as he helped Checo with a tow to slingshot him out of the Ferraris' reach. This was important as Charles Leclerc had to get ahead and stay out in front of Perez to snatch second place in the Drivers' Championship. Early data showed that the Red Bull cars had the edge this weekend, as practice and the qualifying sessions showed a superior pace.

As the sun started to set on the season, it also lowered over the track. Strategies were still being cast, with points on the line as teams and drivers jockeyed for the best finish possible. If you were brave, it was possible a one-stop call could be made; the sensible option, though, was a two-stop. This could be a case of who would blink first. The Red Bull cars both ripped off the line and Perez was tiptoeing ahead but the line was held by Verstappen. The red Ferraris followed with Leclerc slipping into third, but Sainz was surprised by the quick start of Hamilton, who nabbed fourth place. Still on the first lap and looking to get ahead in the points race, Leclerc saw a gap inside Perez, and feinted a move that he couldn't carry through, and now Hamilton was closing fast, with Sainz firmly back in the pack. It was fast as they flicked through the first chicane and Hamilton for a brief moment had all four wheels in the air as he bumped over the kerbs and just about held it together to keep Sainz behind him.

The Red Bulls were inching away and leaving the rest to fight over the minor positions. Leclerc could settle a little as Hamilton ceded his place when a possible penalty loomed. He had gone off the track after his bump, and only held position by running over Turn 7, so he was instructed to give Sainz the place. With the Mercedes now off his tail, the Monegasque driver found his rhythm. The front order now in a groove, it was the next phase of the race and tyre management. Verstappen was clear of Perez, who had the same distance between him and Leclerc, and Sainz was equal distance from his team-mate. The only difference now was that George Russell was up into fifth. With the Hamilton car now handling poorly, he couldn't compete with his young compatriot, who, after a poor start off the line, was still flying after his Brazil victory. It was all good, clean, fair racing, the six lead cars showing that the sum of their parts could entertain under the new rules.

Sainz was struggling to keep up with the front three, and in dropping back he was also keeping the Mercs at bay. The race started to fall away from Russell though, as after his first stop he was released into the path of Lando Norris, and was to pay the price with a penalty. It wasn't helped by the fact his actual stop was slow. The race day for the Silver Arrows wasn't a happy one eventually, as after the highs of Interlagos, they had a DNF with Hamilton, as towards the end of the race his car spluttered with hydraulics issues.

As the two limped around, they could only reflect on the poor W13 that Toto Wolff was happy to see the back of. Did I mention back? Well, the sore ones of the drivers were not as bad as they had been at the midpoint of the year, but they would shudder at the thought of it, bringing back the ghosts of those jarring races. Because of their poor form, and the inadequacies of Sainz, it was all eyes on the lead three and what order they would appear on the podium. With Verstappen in the clean air with an empty track ahead of him, Perez and Leclerc were free to have their personal duel for second on the track and in the standings. Ferrari had made some changes after the practice sessions had shown they were slower than their rivals, and now in the race those tinkering hours were starting to pay off. Checo was starting to get some early tyre degradation and this led to the first pit stop of the trio – opting for a hard set, to offset coming in early, as Leclerc would stay out racing for another half a dozen laps. When he came in, he also went for the harder compound, and the order fell back to as it was, with Max changing his set between the pair.

Leclerc now had to chase, and this would mean losing his tyres quicker than the front pair, but he had no option. Blessed with just one more set of hards going into the race, Verstappen was on a one-stopper; he was the brave one then. His team-mate had a second set so had that choice if he needed to make it. In keeping a distance on Leclerc, Perez was running close enough to Verstappen to feel the strain of the dirty turbulent air swirling behind him.

This meant that his hunter was gaining ground. The Ferrari pit wall then pulled a fast one with a feint in the pit lane for a stop; this led the Red Bull team to react and bring Perez in for another set of hard boots. It was the first time in a long time that Ferrari had won the strategy battle as now their man was clear on the track and just had to manage his tyres to seal second place.

The Red Bull had to get past Hamilton first before even attempting to have a go for Leclerc. This first task was to prove his undoing as it was taking far too long to get past and therefore taking too much out of his tyres. When he finally did get past with DRS help, he was close to ten seconds off Leclerc but on fresher tyres and Leclerc locked in a zone of concentration that meant switching off his radio. The race was back on. It was under three seconds with two laps left. There's nothing like a back-marker race to spoil the momentum though, and when Gasly and Albon were bickering over out-of-points positions, the former took a few corners too many to adhere to the blue-flag warnings. Ultimately this led to Perez's third-place finish in the race, under two seconds separating them, and the same in the standings by three points. 'It was really tricky. Especially at the end of the stint on the hard, even though we had good management.

It was a really perfect execution from our side,' said Leclerc afterwards. They couldn't boast that often in this season where they claimed second in the Constructors' Championship too.

McLaren had a double-point finish but it wasn't enough to get above Alpine. That was even with Alonso retiring from the race with a water leak. It was Ricciardo's last race for the team so perhaps fitting that he had something to show for it. 'Happy and relieved,' he said afterwards, that infectious smile still beaming, even though it was a season to put way behind him and regroup for the future. 'It exemplifies the unflagging enthusiasm and determination he's shown this year,' team principal Andreas Seidl commented after the race.

For McLaren, it had been a mixed season, but they fell short of where they wanted and perhaps should have been. Norris did finish ahead of the sole Alpine on the track at the end, Ocon pushing the Brit all the way, 'It was close.' Just a second between the two at the end, a happy Norris said, 'I just shot my mediums too quickly and his medium-hard-hard seemed a better strategy.' Sebastian Vettel ran his last race, and he finished with a point. His one-stop plan was strong and he held onto his first-stint mediums longer than anyone else, but this backfired and even though he was fighting for higher places at the end, it could've been so much more. It was an expectedly emotional Vettel after the race: 'It was absolutely the wrong strategy, so it is a shame. We were going backwards. I was really trying. I gave it all I could. I feel a bit empty to be honest, it's been a big weekend. Overall it's been a big day and a big thank you to all the support. So many flags, so many smiling faces, which has been very, very special. I'm sure I'm going to miss more than I understand right now.' He epitomised everything a champion driver should be. Controlled aggression, ferocious appetite for winning, and humble. Very humble.

PIT STOP 1

With the amount of rain-affected races this season, the FIA were keen to think through new ideas to resolve issues for drivers regarding visibility. One such innovation could be the use of wheel arches to prevent excessive spray and would be a temporary fit for use when wet tyres were mandatory. Early studies show that spray could be reduced by as much as 50%. Covers would be fitted at the start of a wet race, or during a red flag when a decision could be made, and then stay on even if the race turned dry. This would not be ready until late in the 2023 season but would likely be introduced in the 2024 campaign.

PIT STOP 2

There was much consternation when Max Verstappen would not let his team-mate through to gain extra points in the Brazilian GP. Sergio Perez was left saying Max had shown his true colours, and this led to a team meeting to clear the air between the two. Verstappen had hinted that his decision was borne out of something that had happened earlier in the season, where at Monaco a mistake from Checo led to Max aborting his flying last lap in qualifying. This prompted some to ask if this was a deliberate act, which seemed absurd, and the FIA agreed. No official complaint had been made then, or now, and so FIA president Mohammed Ben Sulayem, who wasn't against pursuing issues, said it was time to draw a line under it all. Red Bull had not, according to Perez, conducted their own investigation into the street race Q3 crash.

RACE RESULTS

	Driver	Team	Time
1.	Max Verstappen	Red Bull	1hr 27m 45.9s
2.	Charles Leclerc	Ferrari	+8.7s
3.	Sergio Perez	Red Bull	+10.0s
4.	Carlos Sainz Jnr	Ferrari	+24.8s
5.	George Russell	Mercedes	+35.8s
6.	Lando Norris	McLaren	+56.2s
7.	Esteban Ocon	Alpine	+57.2s
8.	Lance Stroll	Aston Martin	+1m 16.9s
9.	Daniel Ricciardo	McLaren	+1m 23.2s
10.	Sebastian Vettel	Aston Martin	+1m 23.8s
11.	Yuki Tsunoda	AlphaTauri	+1m 29.3s
12.	Zhou Guanyu	Alfa Romeo	-1 lap 19.0s
13.	Alexander Albon	Williams	-1 lap 19.9s
14.	Pierre Gasly	Alpha Tauri	-1 lap + 20.5s
15.	Valtteri Bottas	Alfa Romeo	-1 lap + 29.7s
16.	Mick Schumacher	Haas	-1 lap + 44.0s
17.	Kevin Magnussen	Haas	-1 lap + 50.7s
18.	Lewis Hamilton	Mercedes	55 laps - hydraulics
19.	Nicholas Latifi	Williams	55 laps - electrical
20.	Fernando Alonso	Alpine	27 laps - water leak

Fastest Lap – Lando Norris 1m 28.3s

Final Drivers' Championship Standings

1.	Verstappen	454pts
2.	Leclerc	308
3.	Perez	305
4.	Russell	275
5.	Sainz	246
6.	Hamilton	240
7.	Norris	122
8.	Ocon	92
9.	Alonso	81
10.	Bottas	49
11.	Ricciardo	37
12.	Vettel	37
13.	Magnussen	25
14.	Gasly	23
15.	Stroll	18
16.	Schumacher	12
17.	Tsunoda	12
18.	Zhou	6
19.	Albon	4
20.	Latifi	2
21.	De Vries	2

Final Constructors' Championship Standings

1.	Red Bull	759pts
2.	Ferrari	554
3.	Mercedes	515
4.	Alpine	173
5.	McLaren	159
6.	Alfa Romeo	55
7.	Aston Martin	55
8.	Haas	37
9.	AlphaTauri	35
10.	Williams	8

FROM A CERTAIN POINT OF VIEW

The Broadcaster

Simon Lazenby is the lead presenter of Sky Sports F1 television coverage. For close to 25 years he has been at the front of much of the broadcaster's sports coverage, including cricket, golf and rugby. 'Sky had all the rights to the England internationals, British Lions tours and Premiership, the Heineken Cup, then Sky got the F1 gig, and my boss moved to F1 and brought me across with him, and I've been doing it ever since and loving it – institutionalised now! It's one of those things that it's as much a lifestyle as it is a job and you either love the travel or you don't, and I've always travelled so I love being on the road and then the time back home as I've got quite a young family [two children under ten] so it can be disruptive, but they've never known anything other than me travelling.'

Over the course of the last decade or so since covering the sport, there have been a lot of changes, and most for the better he explained, '*Drive to Survive* [*DTS*] has changed the paddock enormously, but a number of things have changed the sport. Bernie [Ecclestone] did a fantastic job when he was around but the sport needed to modernise and move on and what Liberty have brought in is that. They know how to market the product and one of the keys was Sean Bratches who was head of marketing for them, and he was the one who worked with Box to Box to get *DTS* off the ground and they've done a great job in bringing it [the sport] to a new audience, and we know that it's had a knock-on effect, along with the racing and our coverage. Those three things have worked together and moved it in the right direction. Our viewing figures are way up, we are seeing exponential growth and it's a result of that, it's changed the pattern for the better. I've never seen paddocks busier or seen races with these sort of [attendance] numbers and also the demographic is younger. We've noticed it's skewed more towards females than ever, and it's younger, with so much online chat about it with social media, which has helped.'

That said, the increasing number creates other issues for broadcast teams, not that it's a real chore, but some are favoured more than others. 'The ones where the paddock is close to the hotel, they're often the ones we love going to! You don't want to spend time travelling around to get to circuits which was fine during the Covid season as there was no fans, but with the sorts of numbers we're seeing it can be quite tricky. There are ones that are more so than others, Mexico City and Brazil is just because of the size of the cities and the traffic, you can't get anywhere in a hurry, but they are great races. Brazil is my favourite circuit – Interlagos. As far as a weekend is concerned and having friends come across, I always say come to Budapest as it's just a terrific city and has had some decent races recently and at the same time it's held at a good time of year and it's just a fabulous city to enjoy. Singapore's also good.'

After Covid and the spike in popularity, the venues were now hitting new records for attendance. 'There's nothing better than going to a sporting event where it's packed and everyone is addicted to the sport, and they are. F1 fans are some of the most committed I've encountered in the years I've been covering sports. They are absolutely passionate; it's been brilliant. There is a thing where it has become a little bit toxic both online and at events; the hysteria around everything that happened in Abu Dhabi has meant you're either in the Max or Lewis camp. No one likes to see and hear booing but at the same time it's got more like football, that's what I've noticed now. You go to the Dutch GP and Lewis is jeered, and at the British GP Max and Christian Horner are. No one likes to see that but it does show that it is a real partisan sport now. I don't think it's bad, but occasionally it crosses the line. Great in terms of the numbers and interest in the sport, but do we want it to become vitriolic? I think we need to watch it and manage it a bit.'

Looking forward, and after a near decade of dominance by the Mercedes team, they have been knocked off top spot by Red Bull. Will this continue? 'I don't think Red Bull will be dominant because Mercedes are such a capable organisation. It was a dog of a car they produced in 2022 and they know it. They put it in the foyer at Brackley, or so Toto [Wolff] says, to inspire how not to make a car for this year [2023]. If they had gone back to the drawing board, which they'll have to, in terms of fundamentals of the design of that car they know it was one thing that they are pointing to that cost them. The porpoising, and the fact they couldn't run it so low; if they've got that right, and I expect them to get it right, I think we could be in for an absolute epic year like we had in 2021. We all want to see them fighting at the front, and the top three teams if they're close and Ferrari get their house in order, we could have a brilliant season in 2023.

Fundamentally it's all down to car design and if Mercedes get on top of it and Ferrari can right their operational errors, there's no reason why this couldn't be a glorious era. It could be one of the eras in F1 history. The cost cap is helping, tapered wind tunnel time, it's all pointing towards making it more competitive and I think that's what Liberty and the sport want to try and make it – a level playing field.'

The ever-changing landscape of Formula 1 means new locations, but it is still the tried and tested ones that come out on top for Simon. 'We're all looking forward to Vegas! They will get it right, but Miami had a few teething problems and it's a destination venue, and it was a very different crowd; it will be the same with Vegas. I think it's people that like to be seen and being there, but at the same time you couldn't get a more iconic backdrop, the fact they're racing down the strip at night is going to look amazing. That's one of the things that works so well with Singapore – that it's just such a dramatic backdrop, like a film set, you see the helicopter shots of Singapore, and it's just like "Wow, that's amazing."'

One of the most entertaining parts of a Sky Sports race weekend broadcast is that of the now-infamous Martin Brundle grid walk. A ceremonious 20 minutes that fills the time between the cars lining up on the grid, and the start of the official proceedings that include the national anthem, and eventual lights out. 'It's a love–hate relationship [he has] with it because he's such a professional. A lot of things are beyond his control, and as a broadcaster that's difficult to handle, but I've got so much respect for him as he takes himself out of his comfort zone every time he does it, and that's why it's so popular. It's the reactions he gets to it, they are so varied; so you can be in Miami, and you'll get a social-media influencer who tells him as such, and he says "Oh, you're modest as well" – it's the genuine general reaction to the weird and wonderful people that turn up on the grid. It's most accentuated in America because you get some quite wacky characters that get on there, it's one of the defining moments of our race weekend coverage and it's iconic, so he knows that we know that, so that's why we love it and it's here to stay, no doubt about that. Compared to the days with Bernie, the grid was extremely exclusive and you had to handwrite a letter to him – I had to handwrite a letter to him to get my wife a paddock pass – and he would vet absolutely all of them. If he didn't think you were worthy, you wouldn't get one, whereas now it's a full paddock. They want it to be full and look vibrant, and it is jam-packed every race.'

Over many seasons there have been many characters surrounding the sport but, as he looks back, Simon recognises that the race is just one part of a driver's make-up, and he recalls a moment that will not be repeated. 'In Canada there were seagulls on the track and there was Sebastian Vettel and Lewis Hamilton, I think I was talking to Lewis in the paddock and Seb came over and started talking about the seagulls and how he had to slow for them – I just let them go, and they were chatting about these seagulls, and it was good fun. They're great lads with so much respect for each other and I like those two. They've done a lot for more than just the sport in recent times as well. Championing different causes.' With Vettel now retired from racing, it's moments like this amongst all the chaos that bring home just how human the drivers and teams are, and without them our race weekends just aren't the same.

The Journalist

Motorsport journalist Ben Hunt started his career as a freelancer in 2002: 'I started working for Wimbledon News having gone through university completing a post-grad in journalism and then worked for different agencies. The Formula 1 job for my current employer *The Sun* started in 2012, and a lot has changed in that time, with Bernie [Ecclestone] in charge, and now Liberty, it has seen a popularity boom through *Drive to Survive* and other media. We had the BBC and

Sky sharing television coverage, so from a newspaper perspective that's good as competition is healthy. The TV coverage was great, and both worked really hard with different features, as well as race coverage; from a personal point of view in the press, we had big Fleet Street representation. *The Mirror*, *Express* and *The Star*, as well as me, *The Mail*, *Telegraph*, *Guardian* and *Times*, so we were quite a big organisation, a collective group. Since then things have changed and there's been fewer staff journalists – myself, *Times*, *Mail* and *Telegraph* that go full-time to the races now. Of course, the BBC TV coverage has gone, it's just radio. Access has also changed. When I first came in I was very surprised by the level we had. We would have sit-downs with Lewis and Jenson at McLaren every week, we'd have 20 minutes with both of those as part of a Fleet Street session. Those have since gone and now it's en masse with the press conferences and if it's decent, Sky will take it live anyway.'

This is where Ben perhaps rues the changes that have been made, as work becomes more difficult, 'I do have an axe to grind with that it's unfair as we travel the world; okay, I'm fortunate that my employer picks up the cost of the travel, but if you're a freelance journo and you're spending thousands to get to Melbourne to ask a question which is then being broadcast live, your main rival blogs are able to pick up the news, twist it around, put it on their site even before you've got back to your desk! So not massively fair if you ask me but it's the beast we're operating in now. You only get a closed session if you arrange your own thing; you can get your share of exclusives, but you've got to work a little bit harder for them.'

With the *Drive to Survive* show already mentioned, Ben had mixed feelings about their contribution, especially behind the scenes. 'From an operational view they never really came to us to tell us what they were doing, and I was hung out to dry on one episode. It was involving Toto Wolff and we'd had a discussion during the season, and then he came up to me and said, "Have you seen it [the episode]?" I told him no. He said they'd covered an exchange that we had; he was pulling my leg a little on it, but no one had come to me from Netflix or Box to Box films to ask if they could use it. I just thought as a matter of courtesy they could've done that. They are very sneaky in what they do as you can be having a conversation, it may be amongst journos, or a driver or whatever, and all of a sudden they'll drop a microphone in above your head. You have to be on your toes, the conversation could've been about dinner the night before, or a driver moving, or a story you're working on, and that fly-on-the-wall access I get, it makes good TV, but I don't want to be falling foul of this. I watched it happen to a friend of mine. A Dutch journalist, he asked a question, and he was filmed, it was a perfectly reasonable question, but of course his picture goes around the world, and with trolls sending him horrible messages, so you have to be careful. The other aspect is it's heavily edited, so you don't need to be a genius to know they splice a lot of it together. They'll be footage that will come from one race, and there'll be talking about another race, and for me that's a bone of contention but that's what they do. The final point is that, because of its success, it's created characters and now there are certain people living up to the character that has been built as a result of the show.' The dangers of a reality-type show is that heroes and villains will be created, and in the modern world these can be divisive.

Going around the world covering a sport you love sounds like a dream job and in many ways it is, but the life of a journalist is more than being passionate about the subject you follow, but as Ben has found out it can also be a tiring affair. 'Travel is a pain. There's no reason why it took me 47 hours to get from Gatwick to Amsterdam other than the incompetence of the airlines and the travel industry, and I do moan a bit – on Twitter – but it also highlights the issue we have there. Having said that, my favourite place to go is Austin. It's a super-cool town, I love the American food, I love the music. It's lost some of its lustre now as it's so popular, it's more expensive and not as fun as it used to be in the past but generally that's a good destination to go to. The best track [for me] is either Japan or São Paulo – they are really great tracks, and Japan's a great place to go visit, Brazil probably less so and it's more problematic getting around to airport to hotel to track. My least favourite? Well, Russia's gone so we can't say that but that was up there, Spain is pretty boring if I'm honest, Monaco lends itself to a bit of a tedious race, but the worst track in terms of design is probably Abu Dhabi. It's a shame we end the season there as it's dreary, and it lends itself to bad racing.'

Once there, though, the atmosphere has changed incredibly over the last few years, and now that fans are breaking records when they enter venues, it makes all that travelling worthwhile. 'The whole part of live sport for me is the fans. I worked in football before and it's all about the fan experience, and what we were missing before under the previous owners was that. People are being asked a lot of money to watch cars go around, and there was no real added value. No concerts, few fan zones, no autograph signings. We've now seen a shift to a better experience under Liberty in terms of more added value and fans getting more for their money. It was quite unique that Silverstone used to put concerts on. People would laugh at the acts, but they still did it, and it was something to see, but it's now commonplace and the newer races that come usually dovetail the race with a big concert. One of the big things post-Covid is the demographic. It's a more even split male/female, as previously it was dominantly male, and also younger people now. During Covid it was quite good for those working in the sport as tests were wearisome and led to travelling being difficult to align. Sometimes you needed to have a test within 72 hours of arriving and get the result back, etc. but travel was efficient and cost-effective. Now it's the opposite, but it's great to have fans back. I love hearing the roar when something's gone on as it comes a split second before the TV sees it, so it's happened and then you look and see what they're reacting to. The cars are quieter now, but if you can hear the crowd over the cars it shows they're having a good time and ultimately that's what we're there for. It's a good barometer for the sport and shows how healthy it is.'

Of course, the reason Ben goes around the world is to get to the heart of the action and try to find that nugget that other media may miss, but how easy is it to gain access to teams and drivers? 'All teams and drivers are pretty accessible, but McLaren stand out as they do put on a separate Lando [Norris] session for us and they are very good at sorting stuff out. That said, Red Bull are also very good, and Mercedes are very proactive keeping you in the loop. Those three stand out for me. The mid-pack and lower teams are fighting for so many sponsors and coverage, but don't do as much to help themselves, and that always staggers me that they are reluctant to come up with ideas and events, and generally help you out, but that's up to them.'

Being a British journalist it's good to get press on the home drivers, and with Lewis Hamilton still fighting off the new talent, he is still the number one target for interviews, but what happens when he and other legends retire? 'Lewis's loss will be massive. I don't think there's been any character in world sport that generates so many stories by himself. Everything he does is newsworthy, partly because he's incredibly successful at what he does, but it's what he does off track, having an opinion. It's as simple as that. Ask David Beckham what he thinks about Qatar, and he won't say anything, ask Mo Farah about US politics, and he may not answer, but if you ask those questions to Lewis, he will have an opinion, and say it. He's not afraid to say it. Think back to the anti-racism stuff that he campaigned for, and people would say it's all very well saying that but why doesn't he put his money where his mouth is. Well he is, now he's funding projects that will make a difference. Sebastian Vettel had to be careful as he had clear opinions, but as Aston Martin had a deal with Saudi-owned Aramco as sponsors, there were certain twists there as he could say certain things but couldn't come out and criticise regimes. But what he did do was focus on the environment and that was the right way to go about it, and when he got married his perspective changed more and he was more focused on those things and was tuning out of F1. When he announced his retirement it freed him up further and he had most overtakes last year as he was driving freer and could go for it.'

After such a keenly fought title race in 2021, but a more one-sided year in 2022, what does Ben think the future will be like on the track? 'I don't think Red Bull will dominate, as I think Mercedes will get back to being closer and I think they will win more races next year. I fully expect Red Bull to win the Constructors' Championship next year, but I think it will be tighter. It won't be as easy for Max [Verstappen] as it was in 2022. Ferrari's issue was operational and reliability as they had the faster car, so had they sorted that out they would've won the Championship, so it's no surprise to see them change team bosses and get a new man in to sort that out as the car itself was very good and I hope they're in the mix. To have a good World Cup you need a good Brazil team, and a good

F1 Championship happens when Ferrari are fighting for the title. I'm looking forward to seeing Lando go up against another team-mate and making that team his own, and seeing just how well he can perform within that team. I'm also excited to see how Red Bull respond despite having won the drivers' titles and now constructors', it hasn't been that straightforward. They've had so much criticism from social media and everywhere, it'll be interesting to see how they play it next year from a brand perspective.'

One of the other aspects is seeing new circuits, with Vegas being the newest, but again the travel aspect is quite daunting. 'For me it's a bittersweet thing as I love the end of the year and if I was a fan, I'd be really excited, but as a journo and potentially travelling to all these destinations, it does fill me with dread, because a triple-header split across two continents, which is Austin, Mexico and Brazil, that's never been done before; we've done it in Europe, followed by a couple of days at home, followed by a Vegas race, which is going to be bonkers, and that's back to back with Abu Dhabi, so I just don't know how that's going to affect people as it feels almost like some sort of science experiment to see how much we can take!'

Epilogue

THE 2022 season, in the end, turned into an anti-climax. The much-anticipated duel that was predicted between the champion with, for some, an asterisk by his name and the seven-time champion just failed to happen – largely down to the latter's car being a bouncing machine, as opposed to the smooth, reliable drive under the former's guidance. Max Verstappen backed up his 2021 season, even with its controversial ending, to prove that his is the best of the new generation of talent. A worthy champion that set new records and will look to enhance his reputation further in the coming years.

His nearest challenger at the start of the year, Charles Leclerc, was let down by his car, and by his eagerness to get back in the fight. His maturity will come in that sense and match his undoubted talent. He will, though, need to be helped by a more competent team, something which has rarely been said about

Ferrari down the years, but make no mistake this is a lean spell for the team and to become champions and carry a threat they need to make changes.

Ultimately on race day the buck stops with the team principal. Just as in most team sports, the manager is the one who is in the firing line when things go wrong, and first to take the acclaim when it all goes right. For Mattia Binotto there was far more wrong than right during the 2021 campaign and after four years at the helm it was time to step away. 'I have decided to conclude my collaboration with Ferrari. I am leaving the company that I love, which I have been a part of for 28 years, with the serenity that comes from the conviction that I have made every effort to achieve the objectives set. I leave a united and growing team. I think it is right to take this step at this time, as hard as the decision has been for me.'

The Ferrari principal job is a poisoned chalice. It is one where you are instantly hailed a hero, or just as quickly forgotten, and in 2022 the team had developed a car that looked as if it would be the dominating force. The opening set of races showed great promise and in Leclerc had a driver taking the fight to Max Verstappen. Strategy calls and reliability then started to plague the team, and each moment just built upon the last until there was a wall of errors that were too high to climb over. With the team not having won a constructors' title for well over a decade, the heavy weight that hung around Binotto's neck was now placed upon that of the Alfa Romeo principal.

Freddie Vasseur had spent the last six years heading up the Alfa Romeo team affairs; now he was willing to put his head on the chopping block as the man tasked with turning the red team's fortunes around: 'I am truly delighted and honoured to take over the leadership of Scuderia Ferrari as team principal. As someone who has always held a lifelong passion for motorsport, Ferrari has always represented the very pinnacle of the racing world to me. I look forward to working with the talented and truly passionate team in Maranello to honour the history and heritage of the Scuderia and deliver for our *tifosi* around the world.' Certainly, full marks for saying the right things. Vasseur had just guided Alfa to their best finish in a decade, and would now look to challenge the dominant Red Bull team, something that Ferrari CEO Benedetto Vigna was confident his new man could do, 'Throughout his career he has successfully combined his technical strengths as a trained engineer with a consistent ability to bring out the best in his drivers and teams. This approach and his leadership are what we need to push Ferrari forward with renewed energy.'

The table is now set for the next chapter in the history of F1. With potential new teams coming on board soon, and with new circuits to navigate, the future is still as bright as the many floodlights shining down on a Singapore track; this, despite recent controversies still hanging loosely like dark clouds over Spa. New drivers will aim to impress, and those looking to prevent Verstappen from claiming more titles and records seem to have their work cut out.

One thing for sure is that the drama will never stop, and each and every race weekend we still eagerly await the moment we hear …

'It's lights out, and away we go!'